JAPAN

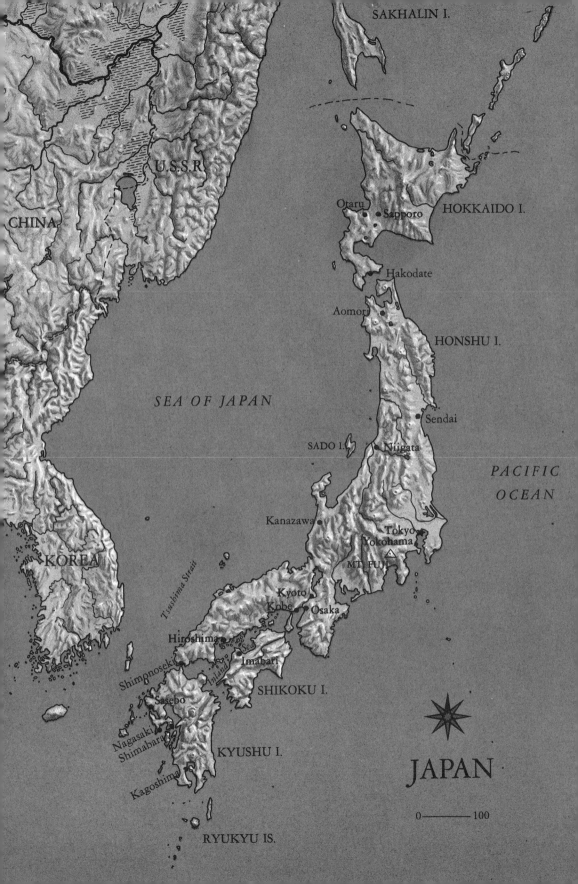

THE HORIZON CONCISE HISTORY OF

JAPAN

by Noel F. Busch

Published by
AMERICAN HERITAGE PUBLISHING CO., INC.
New York 1972

Library of Congress Catalog Card Number: 73-189384
ISBN: 07-009299-0

CHAPTER I

"PARTS OF
THE PICTURE"

J apanese babies don't cry. Japanese mothers carry their children around piggyback from morning to night, tied on by some sort of sash. Japanese children catch crickets and keep them in boxes.

Japanese are more interested in the way food looks than the way it tastes. Instead of cutting it up with fork and knife, they have it chopped up into bite-size pieces beforehand—except that, since it is usually rice, it doesn't even need to be chopped up. Anyway, they eat it with chopsticks, a method they must have picked up from the Chinese.

The Japanese also picked up many other things from the Chinese, including the way they write their own language. This language differs from any other language almost as completely as the Japanese differ from any other people. However, while the Japanese are extraordinarily different from other people, they differ extraordinarily little from each other.

Most Japanese are small, slight, and wiry. None of them has fair hair or blue eyes. They all walk at pretty much the same speed (fast), and they like to do things together. Whatever they do, they do full tilt.

The Japanese are great ones for art. Along with the usual arts, such

Laughing kindergarten children enjoy a school outing.

as writing, painting, and music, they go in for a whole string of special arts of their own, such as flower arranging, tea pouring, and placing rocks in sand.

Sport also appeals greatly to the Japanese, and they do well at games including those they have borrowed from foreigners, like tennis, golf, and baseball. As might be expected, they have odd pastimes of their own. One of these is catching ducks in a net. Another is *judo,* or *jujitsu,* a form of wrestling in which the objective is to make an opponent use his own strength to defeat himself. A third is *sumo* wrestling in which two gigantic Japanese with even more gigantic paunches face each other across a small ring, at the center of which, after prolonged introductory ceremonies, they suddenly collide at top speed.

If all Japanese are about the same small size and shape, how is it that these sumo wrestlers are taller and fatter not only than all other Japanese but also than most other wrestlers? And if other Japanese wrestlers know how to make an opponent use his own strength to defeat himself, why don't sumo wrestlers learn the same trick?

Questions of this kind frequently arise in connection with the Japanese. Nobody knows the answers, least of all the Japanese themselves.

The Japanese have strange thoughts about money. They don't seem to like it as much as people elsewhere. Offer a Japanese taxi driver a tip and he is likely to refuse it with an air of *noblesse oblige.* The head of a Japanese company is often more interested in prestige than in profits and will rarely regard the two as synonymous.

Japanese ideas about religion are also peculiar to them. On the one hand, the Japanese have been addicted to something called Shinto from time immemorial. On the other, they are also addicted to Buddhism in various, and often somewhat esoteric, forms. One out of about 170 Japanese is a Christian. They go in for new and increasingly unintelligible religions of which the latest is called Soka Gokkai. However—except for presumably the Christians—none of these religions seems to include any intelligible sort of God.

Japanese people live in flimsy little wooden houses which are held together, not by nails, but by notches in the beams. The doors of these houses do not swing on hinges but slide from side to side, as do the windows, which may be made out of paper. The floors of the houses are composed of smooth straw mats, and the Japanese sleep on them, instead of in regular beds. Their rooms contain no furniture except for an occasional low table. Instead of sitting in chairs, the Japanese customarily sit on the floor, with their legs folded under them.

Streets in Japanese cities have no names. Japanese people have names but they used to put their first names last and last names first instead of vice versa, the way they are more likely to do now. In an effort to keep such matters straight, all Japanese carry name cards which they like to swap with each other on the slightest provocation.

Japanese are particularly fond of taking baths, especially hot ones. They prefer to do this in company with each other rather than alone. When bathing, a Japanese always scrubs before getting into the tub rather than while in it. The tub is likely to be short, deep, and made out of wood.

The Japanese like little things of various sorts. These include seventeen-syllable poems called *haiku,* antique tobacco-pouch fobs called *netsuke,* dwarf trees called *bonsai,* and transistor radios. The Japanese get great excitement out of the change of seasons, especially the arrival of spring. Trees are of great interest to the Japanese, particularly pine, bamboo, and cherry trees.

Foreigners who visit Japan are forever making up lists like this one of things that the Japanese are, do, like, and so forth. Most such lists, including this one, are thoroughly misleading and serve little purpose except insofar as they suggest that the Japanese are an interesting and enigmatic group. However, stronger substantiation of this point can no doubt be provided by a cross section of widely recognized authorities on the subject.

T*ime* magazine, for May 10, 1971, in a cover story about Japan: "Akira Suzuki, a leading scholar, regards the renowned ambiguity of his country's language as a manifestation of the need that Japanese feel to try to get along with one another. 'If we spoke more clearly to each other,' he says, 'we might end up clashing in fistfights all day long.'"

The late Arthur Waley, widely regarded as the twentieth century's leading Occidental scholar of Oriental languages and its ablest translator into English from both Chinese and Japanese, when informed by a student that she found the Japanese language "dreadfully ambiguous": "Oh really, I have never come across a single case of ambiguity in my whole life."

Anthropologist Ruth Benedict, whose *The Chrysanthemum and the Sword* is regarded by many as the clearest diagnosis of the Japanese character ever written by a foreigner: "The Japanese have been described in the most fantastic series of 'but also's' ever used for any nation of the world. When a serious observer is writing about peoples other than the Japanese and says that they are unprecedentedly polite, he is not likely to add, 'but also insolent and overbearing.' When he says people of some nations are incomparably rigid in their behavior, he does not add, 'but also they adapt themselves readily to extreme innovations.' When he says a people are submissive, he does not explain too that they are not easily amenable to control from above. When he says they are loyal and generous, he does not declare, 'but also treacherous and spiteful.' When he says they are genuinely brave, he does not expatiate on their timidity. When he says. . . . All these contradictions, however, are the warp and woof of books on Japan. They are true. Both the sword and the chrysanthemum are part of the picture. . . ."

Eminent critic Nyosekan Hasegawa in *The Japanese Character, a Cultural Profile:* "The mental and emotional qualities of the Japanese, like those of most highly developed nations, are extremely diverse. . . . They are progressive and at the same time conservative; at one moment they seem to be peace-loving, at another bellicose. Each of these aspects, moreover, is in itself quite strong."

Esteemed scholar and author Edward Seidensticker, American-born translator of contemporary Japanese writers including Nobel Prize winner Yasunari Kawabata: "The Japanese are known as great borrowers, but they are also great preservers. . . . The Japanese are known as the hardest working folk on earth. They also play as hard as they work. . . . The Japanese people are not haunted by the past, but manage to live with it and enjoy it at the same time. . . . But while religion leaves the Japanese unruffled, it has made a deep imprint on their folkways."

Distinguished history professor Kazuo Kawai, in *Japan's American Interlude:* "There does not seem to be any such entity as the 'Japanese soul' or the 'Japanese temperament' which innately predestines the

Subtle ratios and natural materials are keys to the calculated simplicity of these traditional Japanese domestic interiors.

Japanese to any particular pattern of behavior. . . . History can be cited to argue that the Japanese are a revolutionary people as well as to argue that they are a conservative people. The determinant is to be found in the prevailing mood of a particular time, as shaped by the circumstances of the moment."

Townsend Harris, U.S. consul general and minister to Japan, 1855–61: "The lubricity of these people passes belief."

Saint Francis Xavier, Jesuit missionary to Japan, 1549–52: "These people are the delight of my heart."

There is nothing in the least novel about the capacity of the Japanese to please, puzzle, or surprise the rest of the world. They started doing all three when they first appeared on the international scene in A.D. 57 and have continued on an expanding scale ever since. It is therefore only natural that their accomplishments over the last twenty-five years should have been by all odds the most astonishing to date.

On August 14, 1945, when Japan ended World War II by accepting the surrender terms provided by the Potsdam Declaration, its major cities lay in ruin, its industrial plants bombed out, and its people reduced to a per capita income level estimated at the yen equivalent of $27 a year. There seemed to be grave doubt as to whether they would be able to maintain even that abysmally low standard in the future, for post-surrender economic policy, as drafted by the U.S. State, War, and Navy departments, was stern and forbidding: "The plight of Japan is the direct outcome of her own behavior and the Allies will not undertake the burden of repairing the damage."

The dire physical and economic plight in which Japan found herself was exceeded by the misery and confusion of the nation's state of mind. There were sound reasons for this. During the twenty-five hundred years of Japan's recorded history, the nation had experienced only two attempts at invasion by outsiders. Both of these had been made by the Mongols during their brief period of ascendancy in the late thirteenth century, and both had been promptly and effectively repulsed, under conditions which suggested some sort of supernatural assistance.

In 1945, after having been assured by seemingly reliable sources for four years that they were winning a war against the most powerful

Ladies and gentlemen enjoying a bath at the famed spa of Beppu on Kyushu

nations on earth, the Japanese people had suddenly been informed that, on the contrary, the war was over and they had lost. And now, instead of merely being invaded, the country was being occupied by thousands of American soldiers who seemed to feel entirely at home there. The deeply revered emperor was not only himself taking orders from an alien shogun who had installed himself on the top floor of the best office building in Tokyo, but had also instructed all of his subjects to start doing likewise.

In short, a nation which had never before suffered any kind of defeat in war had now suffered one of the most complete and convincing defeats in the whole history of terrestrial warfare. And the United States, having inflicted that defeat, apparently felt no compunction whatsoever about its effect on the victim. Japan's future looked extremely grim and no one understood this better than the unhappy Japanese.

What has occurred in the short span of years since then is that Japan has not merely achieved total recovery, but has reached a level of material prosperity far beyond any envisaged by her leaders even in the event that she had been able to win the war instead of losing it. Between 1945 and 1972, Japan's Gross National Product rose from approximately zero to $200 billion a year, making her the third largest economic power in the world. Meanwhile, annual per capita income jumped from an estimated low of $27 to nearly $2,000—or well above that of most countries in Europe—and is still on the rise. By no means the least amazing feature of this extraordinary performance has been the reaction to it of the Japanese themselves who, far from being awestruck by their own accomplishments, appear to take them all very much in stride.

In 1905 the flagship *Mikasa,* in which Admiral Heihachiro Togo led the Japanese Navy to victory in the battle that decided the outcome of the Russo-Japanese War, was a product of the proud old British armaments firm of Vickers Sons, at Barrow-in-Furness. In 1970 two British trade missions visited Japan in the hope of finding out how their erstwhile customer, having long since replaced Great Britain as the world's biggest shipbuilder, went about the business of mass producing 500,-000-ton oil tankers. Their Japanese hosts welcomed them politely and did their best to explain the procedure.

Golf, like baseball and skiing, reached Japan from the United States, but its proliferation there during the years of postwar affluence has taken unexpected forms. Having built a pair of championship courses near Tokyo, the late newspaper publisher Matsutaro Shoriki added a Disneyland-like outdoor amusement park, for the comfort and convenience of "golf widows" while their husbands were disporting themselves on the links. During World War II, *nisei,* or second-generation Japanese immigrants, in many of America's Western states were rounded up and packed off to concentration camps in a shocking display of race injustice. In 1968, near the Haight-Ashbury district of San Francisco where American hippies were wont to loll and frolic, a joint U.S.-Japanese real estate venture took the form of a Japanese Cultural and Trade Center built around a Japanese-style hotel catering to some twenty thousand Japanese visitors on business or pleasure who pass through that city every year.

Among the questions that arise from developments like these are how it will all end and how it got started in the first place. These, again, are questions to which no one really knows the answers. However, some clues may possibly be provided by a brief glance at the past performance chart.

CHAPTER II

AMATERASU, AND ALL THAT

According to Japanese mythology, the whole business began when a celestial brother-and-sister married couple named Izanagi and Izanami dipped a jeweled spear into the sea. Drops falling from the tip of the spear crystallized into the Japanese islands. A grand-scale master of legerdemain, Izanagi then produced the Sun Goddess, Amaterasu, from his left eye and the Moon God, Tsukiyomi, from his right one. In due course, the grandson of the former, Ninigi by name, came down to earth to supervise developments. Ninigi's grandson, Jimmu Tenno, became emperor of Japan and his descendants have reigned there ever since.

To complaints that such goings on sound a bit unrealistic, the noted eighteenth-century Japanese scholar Moto-ori Norinaga provided a sharp answer. This was that the very improbability of the myth constituted the surest proof of its veracity, since if anyone had invented the story, he would naturally have taken pains to make it plausible. In fact, while it certainly has more elegance and glitter than the somewhat grubby sequence of events alleged to have occurred in the Garden of Eden, the Japanese version of the Creation also seems to contain one or

The mysterious Ainu, aborigines who live on the island of Hokkaido

two elements which do in some respect relate to actuality. To start with, the place where Ninigi is said to have descended was Mount Takachiho on the southernmost Japanese island of Kyushu. As a matter of historical fact, Kyushu is almost indubitably where the early Japanese did put down their first roots.

Less reliable than the place is the time assigned to Ninigi's visitation—660 B.C. according to Western chronology—but even this has some indirect relevance to reality. Perhaps because so many Eastern civilizations—Egyptian, Indian, and Chinese, to mention only the biggest—so noticeably antedate that of Europe, Westerners are sometimes inclined to think that the most Eastern one of all must be one of the oldest. Actually, a salient feature of Japanese culture is that it is all relatively recent; and the main point is not how far it goes back but how fast it has come on. The date of 660 B.C., nonetheless, is much too recent to be credible. The Kyushu equivalent of Genesis must have occurred quite some time before that.

Possibly the best place to start then may be a few billion years earlier, with the geological underpinnings. According to fairly recent findings, the entire Pacific Ocean basin is surrounded by a "ring of fire" composed of volcanoes. This volcanic ring—symptomatic of faulted stratifications liable to cause earthquakes—is actually shaped more like a gigantic arch, starting in Chile, proceeding up the western coast of the Americas to Alaska, and then bending southward through the Kuriles and the Japanese islands to the East Indies, where its renowned pedestal is Java's Krakatoa. Japan, near the apex of the arch, is one of the most precarious points on it for certain reasons which, like so many other things in Japan, are closely linked with Mount Fuji.

Since Fuji is undoubtedly one of the most beautiful mountains in the world, it would have been wholly understandable for Ninigi to have chosen its snow-covered cone as a landing spot—and the fact that he failed to do so suggests that few Japanese had yet reached the neighborhood. However, in the present context, Fuji is interesting less for its beauty than for its height. Usually given as 12,365 feet—possibly because this slightly modest total is easy to remember as being composed of the number of months and then the number of days in the year—this makes Fuji one of the highest volcanoes in the world and one of the highest mountains in Japan, which has many other reasonably high ones. The geological significance of this altitude is that, only a few miles east of Fuji, the world's biggest ocean reaches almost maximum profundity in the Tuscarora Deep—so called because this was the name of the American warship that first took five-mile soundings there.

According to current geological theory, this extraordinary juxtaposition of deep-sea ocean trench and high, volcanic mountain top points up and accentuates the hazardous situation of the whole Japanese archipelago. Even more tangible and visible evidence to the same effect is provided by non-lethal earthquakes, which in Japan occur on an average of twenty a day, and by the numerous other active volcanoes, not to mention the countless hot springs in which the Japanese love to immerse themselves. In fact, the whole chain of islands often seems to be vibrating like a fiddle string while seething like a bowl of tempura on a red-hot hibachi; and newcomers are sometimes inclined to wonder why the whole place does not blow up, break apart, or simply vanish in a puff of smoke.

To the Japanese themselves, the subterranean peculiarities of their homeland are so familiar that they are generally ignored between the intermittent calamities which result therefrom. A more direct and discernible influence upon their national character and behavior than geology has been geography. Like the British Isles on the opposite side of the globe, the four major Japanese islands of Honshu, Kyushu, Shikoku, and Hokkaido form a good-sized (142,000 square-mile) temperate-zone cluster off the coast of the Eurasian land mass. Even more noteworthy than the similarity between the two clusters, however, are certain less conspicuous disparities which may help to account for some of the differences in the behavior of their denizens.

In addition to being relatively stable and devoid of volcanic hazards, the British Isles are largely composed of verdant and gently rolling countryside which, as well as being readily traversible and ideally suited to all sorts of productive cultivation, conceals a warm lining of high-grade coal. The Japanese islands present a totally different aspect. To start with, they are almost devoid of any natural resources whatever except for copious rainfall—of which, however, the beneficial effects are mitigated by the fact that the rain so often arrives in the form of torrents or typhoons. Instead of gently rolling hills, Japan has two ranges of craggy mountains running from north to south which not only divide the east coast from the west, thereby impeding centralization of government or anything else, but also preclude effective agriculture on all but some 17 per cent of the terrain.

Much of this arable scrap is contained in three small alluvial plains, of which the biggest—tucked into a little nook between Fuji and the Tuscarora Deep—is now agriculturally impaired by the presence on it of Tokyo, the world's largest city. A familiar truism of European affairs is that fertile England must export manufactured goods in order to pay for imports of food to sustain its less than fifty million inhabitants. Since infertile Japan now has a population which is just starting to level off at well over a hundred million, it is obvious that the same problem presents itself there in an accentuated form.

One other geographical distinction between the British and the Japanese islands, while less immediately apparent, may have had even more historic significance. This is that, whereas the British Isles are barely twenty-five miles off the coast of Normandy, from which the white cliffs of Dover are clearly visible, Kyushu is more than a hundred miles off the coast of Korea, so that each is invisible to the other across Tsushima Strait. What this relatively trifling difference has meant to Japan among other things is that, while England was being occupied by Romans, Danes, and Normans, the Japanese during the same period of time were never successfully invaded and were seriously menaced only once prior to the year 1945.

The more forbidding nature of the water crossing between Japan and the Asian continent was not, of course, the only reason she was left so much to herself. Another was that unlike Europe, the Asian mainland was tenanted not by a rabble of warring crannies but by the huge and complacent "Middle Kingdom" of China which did not need or wish to be bothered with trifling offshore forays. The net result was that, unlike the British, the Japanese were never subjected to a series of abrupt and compulsory changes in life style, imposed by outsiders whose own life styles differed markedly from each other. On the contrary, once the Japanese had subdued the aboriginal inhabitants of their islands, they were entirely free to adjust to their unique surroundings according to their own inclinations. This they proceeded to do to an extent perhaps unequaled by any other major nation in history.

Oni, or devils, take many different guises: some are women transformed through their own jealousy; here an Oni is disguised as a begging monk.

One final geographical point about Japan often emphasized nowadays by military commentators is that, just as the British islands screen the northeast coast of Europe, thus enabling Britain to blockade the Continent, the Japanese islands even more effectively screen the whole east coast of Asia. In the current stage of world communications, this is unquestionably a point of major significance; in the distant past, however, when blockades were uncalled-for and the only threat offered by the whole wide Pacific was the distinctly remote one of attack by outrigger canoes from Hawaii, it was much less significant. More to the point was that, just as the British Isles, prior to the accessibility of the new world, represented a final cul-de-sac for westward-faring migrants from the Continent, the Japanese islands even more permanently and more completely represented the last stop for all travelers headed east.

Assuming, as seems reasonable, that man originated somewhere more or less near the center of the Afro-Eurasian land mass, it is perhaps not altogether fanciful to suspect that there may be some inherent psychological difference between those elements of the species that worked their way eastward and those that followed the sun toward the west. Obviously most major migrations were governed primarily by practical necessities; nonetheless, migrations toward the setting sun may have had some element in them of adventurous inquiry into what comes next, while those to the east may betoken a converse interest in origins and derivations. Without getting involved in metaphysics, it seems fair to say that Westerners often sense some element of innate traditionalism in Oriental philosophy and religion that is missing in their Western equivalents. And if this element does exist in Oriental philosophy, it surely must be to some extent either a) the result of travel to the East, b) what motivated their travel in the first place, or c) a combination of both.

In any event, it hardly requires a profound grasp of the historical theory of challenge and response to suspect that the advance guard of the eastward-faring peoples, on finding itself trapped more or less incommunicado on a scenically enticing but agriculturally inadequate minefield of eruptions and convulsions, might well develop a few special characteristics not shared by fellow mortals reared in more congenial and less isolated circumstances. Perhaps then, the marvel is not that the Japanese differ in some respects from the rest of mankind but that they are, in most essentials, so much like the rest of us.

While few historians since the time of Moto-ori have attempted to make a serious case for the Ninigi-Jimmu Tenno theory of Japan's origin, the sad truth is that none of them has yet produced an altogether satisfactory substitute. The consensus nowadays is the eminently plausible one that most of the earliest settlers of Kyushu arrived by sea from the southern tip of Korea. In the considerable volume of archaeological evidence for this belief, one ingredient alone is perhaps sufficient to substantiate it. This is that some of the later arrivals brought with them bronze mirrors, straight swords, and jewels in the shape of a claw—three items which still form the essential elements of the imperial regalia—and which are identical with early counterparts found on the mainland. Nonetheless, while doubtless fundamentally sound, the theory is not immune to one or two nagging objections.

One objection is that, if Tsushima Strait served to preclude later attempts at conquest, it seems odd that it did not also dissuade prehistoric migrants from making the passage in fairly large numbers. Part of the answer here may be that some of the earliest arrivals were accidental ones; and also that, when the first settlers reached Kyushu from the mainland, there was practically no one there to keep them out. It seems probable too that the earliest migrants came across in small installments and at different times over a fairly long period.

A second and somewhat more puzzling flaw in the theory concerns the Japanese language. If the later migrants from the mainland could bring bronze gadgets like mirrors and swords, one might have expected them also to have imported some dialect of Chinese or Korean, which, in fact, they notably failed to do. On the contrary, the language they did bring bears little relation to any other known tongue, with the remotely possible exceptions of Hungarian and Finnish. Its questionable similarity to both might seem to imply some sort of explosive migrations by prehistoric tribes speaking some primitive patois, of which these three are distant derivatives, but only the flimsiest evidence has so far turned up to support this belief. Some linguists have proposed that Japanese may derive from some now defunct East Indian vernacular brought to Japan by aboriginal immigrants from the south who reached Kyushu

OVERLEAF: *Japan is a land of great physical contrasts, from its rocky coast to its snow fields, volcanic craters, and placidly beautiful Inland Sea.*

by island-hopping through the Ryukyus and were then absorbed by later arrivals. Here too, however, the clues are far from verifiable; the origins of the Japanese language are still a mystery and seem likely to remain so.

If, instead of linguistic clues, architectural ones are sought for the origin of the Japanese, the South Sea Islands hypothesis gains some modicum of credibility. While Japanese architecture during historic times has been considerably affected first by Chinese and later by Western influences, the original dwellings in Japan seem to have followed more or less the designs of those found on the islands to the south or even on the Malay Peninsula. However, light wooden houses assembled over a mortised framework would in any case have been well suited to a land where wood was plentiful and where earthquakes were likely to demolish masonry structures more completely and with more lethal effects. Hence, there are also grounds for supposing that Japanese building styles were largely an indigenous invention—or simply an adaptation of similar rudimentary styles also found on the continent.

In sum, a reasonable guess as to what actually happened is that successive waves of immigrants, some perhaps straying north from the South Seas, but many more crossing the straits from the mainland, met and mingled more or less amicably first on Kyushu and later on the main island of Honshu, where in due course they collaborated in concocting a language that eventually ceased to have any discernible relationship to any of its sources. If so, one factor which perhaps encouraged the new arrivals to join forces with each other was the necessity for dealing with resident aborigines whom they termed—apparently with a rather scornful inflection—the Hairy Ainu.

The origin of the Ainu, like those of the Japanese themselves, remains mysterious, but the abundant facial hair which the relatively beardless mainlanders found so distasteful suggests—as do the blue eyes still found among their few remaining descendants—that they were some displaced strain of Caucasian. They had apparently reached Honshu, via Sakhalin and Hokkaido where a few hundred surviving families nowadays still constitute a somewhat dubious attraction for tourists. Whether the Ainu ever got as far south as Kyushu seems doubtful, but they were apparently encountered in increasing numbers

as the newcomers, in search of more fertile lands, pushed north across
Shimonoseki Strait and then eastward on the main island.

Given their monsoon climate and scattered pockets of rich alluvial soil, the Japanese were, like other East Asian peoples, virtually obliged to specialize in wet-rice farming from the start. The three coastal plains where this form of agriculture can best be practiced are those which now surround the cities of Tokyo, Osaka, and Kyoto, and it was in the third and most fertile of these areas, then known as Yamato, that the Japanese established their first major base on the main island of Honshu. The effort to clear the land of Ainu—who lived by hunting rather than farming—intensified as the newcomers reached as far east as the Kanto plain, the site of what is now Tokyo. That the Japanese aversion to the Ainu applied only to the male of the species can be inferred not only from the pejorative adjective which usually precedes the name, but also from the fact that the Japanese themselves are now a good deal more hirsute than their counterparts on the mainland. In any case, they were still engaged in the preliminaries to undisputed possession of Honshu which were to last for the next millennium when they made their official appearance on the historical scene. This took place in the year A.D. 57 in the form of an announcement of the arrival of an envoy from Japan at the Chinese court during the Han dynasty.

To China, the Japanese are indebted not only for their first written mention in history but also for the name by which their own country has since been known therein. First referred to by the Chinese as *wa,* or dwarfs, the Japanese were later on pleased when their native habitat was accorded the designation of *Jih-pen,* or "land of sunrise." In Japan itself this flattering name was adopted with a phonetic twist as "Nippon" to which, as the nation began to expand from the confines of the original Yamato, the syllable *Dai,* meaning "great," was added as a customary prefix. The Chinese name reached Europe first from Marco Polo, whose Italianate approximation was "Chipango," and then through Malaya and the East Indies where it was pronounced more like "Japang" or "Japun."

The lack of contemporary records in Japan corresponding to the Chinese reports of their early embassies can be readily explained. While the Japanese had brought with them from the mainland such recondite skills as metallurgy, silk weaving, and wet-rice growing, they had not yet found time to acquire the knack of writing. For this, they were obliged to wait until the seventh century A.D. when increased traffic with their Chinese mentors had further underlined the political value, the economic convenience, and perhaps above all, the sheer pleasure to be gained from this novel accomplishment.

The failure of the Japanese to bring the art of writing with them helps confirm the view that their first arrival in Kyushu must in reality have far antedated that assigned to the arrival of Jimmu. By 660 B.C. Chinese literature was already several hundred years old, and immigrants from the continent would surely have had ample time to absorb the underlying principles. What may deserve more careful scrutiny, however, is the rapidity with which, once they were properly introduced to the new skill, they took pride and delight in mastering it. In fact, the speed and flexibility of Japanese response in circumstances of this sort whenever they have arisen has been perhaps the key theme of their history as a whole. Certainly it deserves some elucidation beyond the tired cliché with which Westerners have customarily consoled themselves when confronted by Japanese adaptive virtuosity, to the effect that what this really proves is their lack of true "creativeness" in literature and the arts.

Without delving too deeply into the semantics of what "creativeness" actually means—since, after all, such acknowledged creators as Shakespeare, Bach, and Michelangelo never felt themselves obliged to devise new forms for their masterpieces but were quite content to use those already at hand—it may be suspected that this disparagement merely illustrates the familiar principle that the quickness of the hand deceives the eye. Actually, when utilizing a Western invention like writing, just as Shakespeare utilized the blank verse drama, the Japanese did it with a celerity which concealed the creativity of this feat by making it look easy.

What apparently struck the Japanese about Chinese ideographs first of all was a characteristic whose main implications many Europeans, even now, find surprisingly hard to grasp. This is that, while such ideographs were invented for the purpose of expressing Chinese ideas, they can also be used for expressing ideas of any kind. To put this another way, Chinese ideographs, like Arabic numerals, are in no sense anchored to phonetics; and just as the numeral "5," for example,

The deity Izanagi and his goddess Izanami creating land from droplets of water

means five, cinq, or fünf, according to the language in which it is voiced, Chinese ideographs can be voiced in any language whatsoever. In other words, English, French, or German can be written in Chinese ideographs, if not quite as readily as Chinese itself, then at least just as readily as Japanese. If Europeans, when they first encountered Chinese a thousand years later, had responded with the same imaginative enthusiasm and the same willingness to devote a few years of hard work to learning it, Chinese calligraphy might by this time in some simplified form have become the basis of a universally accepted multilingual script with corresponding benefits to all concerned—just as it is now accepted everywhere in China where two persons speaking in vocally differentiated dialects can readily understand each other by outlining characters on the palm of one hand with the forefinger of the other.

In adapting Chinese calligraphy, the Japanese, of course, went much further than, for example, merely using the Chinese symbol for *mao,* an onomatopoeic Chinese word meaning "cat," to represent their own quite different word *neko* meaning the same thing. They combined this system with a kind of shorthand whereby some Chinese ideographs were given a phonetic equivalent in Japanese, thus endowing the latter with some of the advantages of an alphabet without actually possessing one. This highly creative notion of blending two seemingly antithetical methods of writing was long ago vastly elaborated and codified into the *hiragana* and *katakana* symbols with which modern Japanese supplements the basic Chinese. These additives, of course, make it even harder to learn to write Japanese than it is to learn to write Chinese, let alone any European language, since it involves memorizing hundreds of ideographic characters plus at least two phonetic syllabaries instead of a couple of dozen letters.

Even more impressive than the creativity with which the Japanese absorbed Chinese calligraphy was that exemplified in their early excursions into the fresh field of literature. Sir George Sansom in his authoritative *History of Japan* cites an A.D. 890 "Catalog of Books at Present in Japan" to the effect that there were then a mere 1,579 titles and 16,790 volumes in the whole country. Not long before, to be sure, a fire in the palace library had burned a good many others, but nonetheless a total of under 17,000 volumes—less than can nowadays be found

in almost any one of the nation's bookshops—seems significantly modest for a culture already prepared to contribute to world literature
classics likely to last as long as humans retain the ability to read.

Most renowned of the classics of the period is of course the celebrated *Genji Monogatori,* or *Story of Genji,* by Lady Murasaki Shikibu.
This is the engaging chronicle of a young prince, whose travels,
amours, and often misdirected efforts to acquire an education, are
recounted with a light touch and an effortless urbanity which, in Arthur Waley's superb English version, often seems more in the vein of
Marcel Proust than of Lady Shikibu's contemporaries in Europe whose
literary tradition dated back to Homer. However, since quotations
from *Genji* lose their flavor in being taken out of context, the tone of
the period—about the turn of the first millennium, when court life at
Kyoto was at its height—may be more effectively suggested by a selection from the somewhat earlier and almost equally celebrated *Pillow
Book* of Sei Shonagon, as admirably translated by Ivan Morris. Since
the Japanese at that time did not (and even at present usually do not)
use pillows of the European type but preferred wooden or porcelain
headrests, the translated title may be somewhat misleading. What it
means is a collection of night-thoughts, casual reminiscences, and
samples of what, if Japanese houses had stairs, would be *esprit d'es-
calier.* A good many court ladies kept such books, more or less as Vic-
torians kept diaries and daybooks, but Sei Shonagon's small master-
piece differs widely enough from both types to suggest that Japanese
literature had vaulted from the naivete of Beowulf to the sophistication of *The New Yorker,* or perhaps even further, in three centuries
or so. A favorite medium of composition for such books was a list of
things or characteristics liked or disliked:

Things That Lose by Being Painted
Pinks, cherry blossoms, yellow roses.
Men or women who are praised in romances as being beautiful.

Things That Gain by Being Painted
Pines, autumn fields, mountain villages and paths.
Cranes and deer.
A very cold winter scene; an unspeakably hot summer scene.

A visit to a horse race.

Twisting a paper cord for one's hair.

One has gone to a quite ordinary place when suddenly one hears a vaguely familiar voice. This alone is enough to make one nervous; but it is still more disquieting if someone else comes along and begins speaking about that other person.

When a man or woman whom one loathes comes to call, one becomes extremely nervous.

When a man who has spent the night with a woman is late with his next-morning letter, it worries not only the woman herself but even people who hear about the matter.

When a woman produces a letter that she has received from a man one loves oneself, it makes one very nervous indeed.

To jump from the first Japanese Embassy to China in A.D. 57 to Sei Shonagon's memoirs of the court at Kyoto in the closing years of the first millennium A.D. may well seem a bit staccato even for a history which, like Japan's, is chiefly characterized by lightning switches of one sort or another. This is all the more true in that, while Japanese history prior to about the halfway point in the millennium is practically nonexistent, the same subject is thereafter treated with play-by-play exactitude in numerous homemade chronicles which make a typically valiant attempt to outdo their Chinese models for diligence and detail. However, for a treatise like the one in hand, the only way to go about the business is in a sort of rapid-fire chronological style which Western readers may find hard going for two additional reasons.

One of these reasons concerns the kind of names that Japanese history necessarily involves. Just as Oriental faces tend to look alike to Occidentals because each differs from each other less than they all differ from Caucasian faces—and, of course, vice versa—so, too, Japanese names tend to sound alike to Europeans because each name indeed differs less from other Japanese names than they all do from all European names. For example, fewer than a dozen Japanese names have been used in this whole book so far, but the chances are that many readers have understandably got them all mixed up already.

The second disadvantage is an even more peculiarly Japanese one.

In a nation where the divine right of kings was considered not a mere privilege conferred on royalty from far above but rather a direct and inalienable inheritance, the process of governance naturally presented special problems. One of these was that the line of inheritance must never be interrupted—since if it were, the consequent confusion would be total and unimaginable. This in turn meant not only that the divine ruler had to be scrupulously protected at all times, but also that the top ministers who bore this onerous responsibility attained an earthly status which, in nations less closely plugged in to sources of celestial power, was held by mere kings, tsars, and emperors. Hence, long before Japan's celebrated shogunal system emerged in the twelfth century, earlier experimental systems were devised whereby chancellors, regents, and more or less omnipotent prime ministers wielded the authority which, in more mundane governments elsewhere, was vested in the ruler himself. What this means to an Occidental reader of Japanese history is that, instead of a mere single line of kings with familiar names that are already forgettable enough, he is confronted with a long series of two or three more or less simultaneous heads of state, government, or both, whose unfamiliar names seem totally impossible to distinguish even from each other, let alone from those of their predecessors and successors. Very few of them, accordingly, are likely to get off the printed page and into his private file of Things to be Remembered.

Save for the scanty quota available from Chinese sources, Japanese dates prior to around A.D. 500 are, if possible, even less reliable than accounts of the events they are supposed to commemorate. Occasional Chinese references to a "Queen Country" in Japan, however, do tend to confirm later Japanese legends about a somewhat Amazonian empress named Jingo whose armies conquered the southern part of Korea. In any case, from the start of the Christian era to about A.D. 550, it does appear that the area of Yamato, in addition to expanding eastward on Honshu and absorbing another Japanese settlement called Izumo on the west coast of the main island, also acquired some measure of control over the part of southern Korea surrounding what is now Pusan. About the middle of the sixth century, this area, known as Mimana, fell to the kingdom of Silla, its neighbor to the north. At about the same time or shortly thereafter, another event took place in

Korea which was to make subsequent Japanese history both more voluminous and more trustworthy.

During the third and fourth centuries A.D., the teachings of an Indian sage and mystic named Gautama Buddha had been spreading rapidly. By the fourth century, they had reached Korea where they progressed even faster. In A.D. 552 the king of the western Korean kingdom of Paikche, himself embroiled in a war with Silla, dispatched a mission to Yamato asking for military aid and carrying presents which included a bronze statue of Buddha, some scrolls of Buddhist teachings, and a personal letter extolling the new faith. It was this mission which is generally cited by Japanese historians—whose own activities date more or less from the same time—as the beginning of Yamato's long Chinese tutelage, which lasted through the next five centuries.

Whether or not the mission from Paikche really deserves full credit for putting Japan on the course that was so largely to determine its subsequent character remains an unanswered question, but it certainly sparked a major political upheaval which contributed notably to that result. Of the great landed families who were then in contention with each other for the prestigious responsibility of running the Yamato government on behalf of the emperor, two of the most powerful were the Soga and the Nakatomi. The prime responsibility of the Nakatomi was staffing and caring for the shrines dedicated to the Japanese animistic cult which was later to be known as Shinto, or "way of the gods," to distinguish it from the newly imported way of Buddha. When the Nakatomi, for obvious reasons, tried to discourage the new cult, the Soga, for equally understandable notions, were all for building it up. The result was a feud ending in a typical Japanese standoff whereby, after almost a century of sparring, a Nakatomi later to be known as Fujiwara Kamatari took charge of working out a comprehensive overhaul of the entire Japanese governmental system. Using methods and models taken from the T'ang dynasty, this Great Reform of A.D. 645 called for more equitable provisions covering taxation, land tenure, and general administration. As eventually shown, however, its main effects were to encourage rather than suppress the rise of Buddhism and thereby also to accentuate Chinese dominance of Japanese thought, politics, and behavior in general throughout the next three centuries.

The Heian shrine, built in 1895, is a replica of the Imperial Palace of 794.

During the sixth and seventh centuries, frequent official embassies to Ch'ang-an from Yamato were accompanied by able young government officials and students. Many of these stayed on through the interval of years between one mission and the next to delve deeper into the broad array of fine arts, the relatively permissive and equitable governmental procedures, and the rich Confucian philosophy on which all this was based. Carried back to Japan by these emissaries, who sometimes also brought along Chinese tutors to help expound and demonstrate their specialties on the spot, the resultant infusions of mainland culture caused a rapid metamorphosis in the theretofore backward little kingdom of Yamato. As early as the seventh century, a Japanese emperor went so far as to address a memorandum to Ch'ang-an as coming from "The Emperor of the Rising Sun to the Emperor of the Setting Sun." No more pleased at being addressed as an equal by another ruler than was his nineteenth-century successor when Queen Victoria made a gaffe of much the same sort, the recipient ignored it. The result was a coolness between the two regimes which lasted for several decades—without, however, noticeably diminishing the Japanese relish for Chinese importations in the cultural field.

One dramatic manifestation of this ravenous appetite was the completion of the first official Japanese capital at Nara, in the year 710. Theretofore, because Shinto custom frowned upon one emperor inhabiting the same locality in which his predecessor had expired, each ruler had set up his own court in a new locale. When Buddhist doctrine provided a release from this superstition, the consequence was a splendid countryside replica of the T'ang dynasty capital whose massive wooden temples still stand to awe visitors by the scale of the undertaking. Less than a century later, however, even Nara seemed inadequate, and in 794 a far grander capital replaced it a few miles farther north, at Kyoto, then known as Heian-kyo, or "Capital of Eternal Tranquillity." It was there that Japan's emperors were to live for the next thousand years and where court life reached a peak of elegance rarely equaled either in Japan or, for that matter, anywhere on earth before or since.

During the centuries that followed the Great Reform of 645, the descendants of Fujiwara Kamatari, who had founded a separate line under his newly acquired patronym, supplanted all rival clans in influence at court, chiefly by means of petticoat influence. As the Fujiwara clan multiplied into numerous branches, they raised this familiar device to a peak of systematic efficiency which owed a good deal to the science of genetics. As soon as a crown prince of the royal house reached marriageable age, he was paired off with a Fujiwara daughter. When they produced an heir, the same procedure was followed except that, if the crown prince had meanwhile become emperor, he was encouraged to abdicate or retire to a Buddhist monastery. In this case, the new emperor, then often not yet of marriageable age, was provided with a Fujiwara regent to keep him in hand until he was old enough to be equipped with a Fujiwara father-in-law. Since about all the throne could offer an incumbent emperor was a tiresome round of ceremonial duties stage-managed by other Fujiwara in-laws of one degree or another, the royal scions were usually, after impressively short reigns, only too ready to turn the job over to younger and even more docile successors. After a few centuries of this, the sequence of Fujiwara regents had become so firmly established that it looked as though their authority might last as long as the imperial line, or even longer. Such was not to be the case.

During the eleventh and twelfth centuries, the Fujiwara system, which naturally encouraged court socialities, frivolities, and amorous improprieties, obliged nobles who lacked the taste or talent for such pursuits to find other and less enervating lines of work. The most popular of these were posts in the provincial administration charged with subduing the unruly Ainu and maintaining order generally in the northern provinces. From this there developed a new grouping of warrior clans who, while disdained at Kyoto as uncouth frontiersmen, nonetheless possessed certain undeniably useful assets, such as well-trained private armies. Strongest of these clans were the Taira and the Minamoto, both of which owed their ascendancy in part to having been founded in the distant past by collateral branches of the imperial line.

About the middle of the twelfth century, certain bickerings among rival factions at court caused these factions to turn to the country clans for help in settling the squabbles. The result was to crystallize the natural rivalry between the Taira and the Minamoto into a civil war waged with phenomenal ferocity, from which a Taira by the name of Kiyomori emerged victorious in the year 1160. Instead of going back to the woods where the court felt he belonged, Kiyomori moved into Kyoto and settled down there, surrounded by his own captains and counselors. There he took the title of grand chancellor and, in the approved Fujiwara style, married his daughter off to the emperor. The couple produced an heir who soon occupied the throne.

Had Taira Kiyomori exterminated all the top survivors of the defeated Minamoto clan, things might have gone smoothly for him. Instead, he allowed a few members to survive, of whom one, Minamoto Yoritomo, although reared by a Taira-appointed guardian, grew up to be an effective and ambitious opposition leader. Rallying remnants of the Minamoto clan on the east coast, he soon welded them into an army formidable enough to challenge the Taira, who by this time had lost popular support through excesses of enthusiasm in their role as successors to the Fujiwara. Shortly after the death of Taira Kiyomori, the Minamoto struck again; and this time, after another bitterly waged civil war, they routed the Taira in a sea battle at Shimonoseki Strait in 1185. There the Taira boy emperor was drowned and the remainder of the Taira clan—save for a considerable number who had switched sides in the course of the struggle—fled back to the countryside or in their defeated warships southward to the Ryukyu Islands, where some of their descendants still carry on the line.

When related in bald terms, the war between the Minamoto and the Taira, though fought with all the excesses of cruelty, treachery, courage, and commotion customary in civil strife, perhaps has small claim upon the attention, let alone the emotions, of a modern reader. Nonetheless, as can be deduced from more detailed accounts, it constitutes one of the most consequential as well as most colorful chapters in the long and lively history of Japan as a whole. That the war was fought so bitterly and for so long tends to obscure the fact that, in a sense, both factions were on the same side. The real issue was not a difference of policy or position between the Taira and the Minamoto. What had happened was that both had sensed intuitively that a new era was arriving in which the real power of Japan would belong not to the court at Kyoto but to one of the great military families which had grown up in the provinces. Each clan wanted to be the one to wield that power.

Rice fields cultivated under centuries-old methods of irrigation and terracing

Both sides were correct; and the closing years of what historians refer to as the Heian period saw numerous other major developments, including new currents of thought and new acquisition of influence by the Buddhist movement. What most dramatically underlined the basic alteration was Minamoto Yoritomo's behavior after his victory over the Taira. Instead of taking over the role of the Fujiwara regents as Taira Kiyomori had done, he assumed only the title of shogun, meaning commander in chief or generalissimo. Instead of settling down in Kyoto, he retired to a *bakufu,* or "headquarters," near his family seat at the seaside village of Kamakura on the east coast, leaving the Fujiwara and the emperors to go back to their customary routine in the capital.

On the surface this might have seemed to be a graceful, not to say docile, retirement from public affairs. In fact it was precisely the opposite. Thereafter, not Kyoto but Kamakura was the true nerve center of the country, and not the Fujiwara regents but the Minamoto shoguns its real rulers. This truth was underlined by the fact that the shogunate was to become an hereditary office like the throne, and such an important one that within twenty years the shogun, like the emperor, came to require a regent, in his case known as a *shikken.*

Instead of rewarding his close relatives and top captains with honorary titles at court, Yoritomo took a more wary line. This was to reward captains and cousins with meaningful jobs in the provincial administration and to kill off his close relatives, including his brother, although the latter happened also to be his ablest general, lest they be tempted to presume too far on the privileges of blood ties. The result was that, when Yoritomo died in 1199 of injuries sustained when he was thrown by a horse, his closest kin were relatives of his wife whose family name was Hojo. The Hojo promptly moved onto the Kamakura scene in a role analogous to that of the Fujiwara at Kyoto.

The relationship between the bakufu as run by the Hojo shikkens at Kamakura and the emperor's court as run by the Fujiwara regents might have seemed largely vestigial except for one important prerogative still at least nominally preserved by the latter. This was the privilege of naming the shogun; and while, as a matter of practice, this privilege was actually exercised by the Hojo family, they were usually discreet enough to select as shogun a member of either the Fujiwara

or the imperial family. However, the fact that the unpretentious little
seaside headquarters at Kamakura, ostensibly set up like the mere
household office of a rich provincial nobleman, really had more leverage than the court at Kyoto escaped no one's attention. In short order
this shift produced far-reaching changes in every aspect of Japanese
affairs.

From the founding of the bakufu regime dates a whole new
Japanese approach to life—as though, in ancient Greece, the decline
of Athens had been followed by a complete and lasting transfer of
spiritual leadership to Sparta. Thereafter, in what came to be known
as the Kamakura period, elegance, good manners, and a true sense of
discrimination in the fine arts were less in demand than courage,
swordmanship, and loyalty to one's chief on the battlefield. Literature
itself experienced a complete metamorphosis. Instead of pillow books
and sophisticated novels, what was needed—and in copious quantities,
supplied—were epics, war stories, and dramatic renderings of battles
between the Minamoto and the Taira. In short, Japan became almost
overnight the militaristic society which, with occasional modification,
it was to remain for the next seven centuries. And this change came
not a moment too soon, for what the nation was about to encounter
was the most alarming challenge in its entire history prior to that
provided by the United States in 1945.

CHAPTER III

THE
WARRIOR'S
DREAM

While Japan was growing from what was the tiny enclave of Yamato into a more or less cohesive nation, comprising the warriors of Kamakura at one extreme and the dilettantes of Kyoto at the other, affairs on the Asian mainland were by no means standing still. There, the resplendent T'ang dynasty had been replaced by the Sung which, in the early twelfth century, lost the northern provinces to a new power which swept down from the western steppes to dominate not merely the Far East but eventually most of the civilized world. This was the "Golden Horde" of Mongols from northern Asia whose later leaders, Genghis Khan and his grandson Kublai Khan, conquered most of their home continent and a good-sized chunk of eastern Europe in the course of the next two centuries. Toward the end of these gigantic operations, Kublai Khan, having annexed Korea, took note of the existence of Japan. In 1268, he dispatched an embassy thereto with a message saying that he was prepared to accept homage from the local king, on pain of prompt invasion. Presented first to the bakufu at Kamakura, this message was in due course forwarded to the imperial court at Kyoto where it created grave consternation.

A masked Shinto priest performs the ancient bugaku *dance. It tells the story of a gentle-faced prince who wore a dragon mask to give his army courage.*

Rumors about the Mongols that had already reached the capital from Korea and South China suggested that the khan's threat called for a tactful and conciliatory reply. Several weeks were spent in drafting one which was then returned to the bakufu for approval and dispatch. What occurred thereafter showed how much things had changed since the era of the Fujiwara regents. The message, which might well have led to a summit conference, whereby Japan would have been reduced to a vassal state like Korea and China itself, was never sent. Instead, with a sound intuition for the realities of the situation, the bakufu had the Mongol envoys packed off with no reply whatsoever. This was tantamount to an invitation to make war—and one which the Mongols could be counted on to accept.

Already in possession of a greater expanse of territory than that acquired by either Alexander the Great or Rome under Trajan, the Mongol emperor could hardly have been expected to give the conquest of a little offshore principality like Japan a very high order of priority. Furthermore, since amphibious operations were a wholly new line of endeavor for the Mongol armies, which had theretofore relied largely on cavalry blitzkrieg, it involved employing the services of the Koreans, who were Asia's master mariners of the period. While all this led to substantial delays—during which a second embassy to Japan was dismissed with even less ceremony than the first—a huge fleet was finally assembled and put to sea in November, 1274. Made up of some 25,000 Chinese, Korean, and Mongolian troops carried in eight hundred vessels, this formidable armada reached the port of Hakata on the nineteenth of the month. There the invaders—having already seized the offshore islands of Tsushima and Iki on the way over— took several outlying villages and proceeded to attack the town.

To the Japanese, whose martial traditions called for singlehanded combat between knightly warriors, the Mongol mass formations came as an effective surprise. After a day of furious fighting, the hastily assembled defending force was thrown back several miles inland, and it appeared that all it could hope to do thereafter was fight a delaying action until reinforcements had time to arrive from other parts of Kyushu and the main island of Honshu. Here, however, nature took a hand in the operation in a way which was to have far-reaching effects on subsequent Japanese history. The sailors on the Korean vessels which had landed the invading force were well aware of the dangerous vagaries of autumn weather in the Tsushima Strait. Now, in what proved to be a stormy night of wind and rain, the senior captains read the signs of an approaching typhoon which would batter their ships to pieces on the rocks. They succeeded in convincing the Mongol commanders of the ground forces that the only hope of saving their men was an immediate return to the boats followed by hasty departure. Resigned to a last-ditch defense to hold the invaders at bay, the Japanese were amazed and delighted when, instead, at dawn the next morning, they saw the last of the Korean ships sailing out of the harbor, headed for home.

While the initial assault by the Mongols had been satisfactorily turned back, it still left the Japanese under dire threat. No one had the least doubt that the invaders would return; and the first taste of battle with them had by no means been altogether encouraging. In addition to their superiority in formation fighting, the Mongols had a distinct edge in weaponry which included an early form of gunpowder bomb, propelled by catapult. Moreover, in arriving by sea, an invading army would have the advantage of initial numerical superiority since it could pick its landing place while the defenders had to man outposts along an extended section of the coast. Suspecting that when the Mongols returned they would do so in vastly increased numbers, the Japanese had little doubt of what they would be up against.

In a situation comparable to that of Nazi Germany while awaiting the Allied invasion of 1944, the bakufu reacted in much the same way. Defenses analogous to those of Hitler's Atlantic Wall were constructed along the southwestern coast. Command posts were manned by the ablest and most distinguished warriors in the nation, including members of the Hojo clan itself. In 1275 the Great Khan, understandably astounded that the Japanese could feel themselves capable of resisting a power that had already overwhelmed most of the known world, sent a final embassy to give the enemy one more chance to knuckle under. This time the Kamakura bakufu, instead of merely sending its members back without an answer, underlined the point by having all six of them summarily beheaded.

In their belief that this time the Mongols would come in greater

OVERLEAF: *The burning of the Sanjo Palace on January 19, 1160, provoked the Heiji war, a power struggle between the Fujiwara clan and the imperial family.*

numbers and prepared to stay longer, the Japanese were by no means mistaken. Convinced by their treatment of his envoys that the islanders merited punishment of the sternest sort, the Great Khan set about preparing it for them with painstaking deliberation, by appointing a special "Office for the Chastisement of Japan." Having now completed the conquest of Sung China, he had at his disposal all its ships as well as its defeated armies. In addition, the vassal king of what was by this time known as Koryo, embracing all of the Korean peninsula and some territory to the north of it, was an eager instead of a reluctant ally. Seeing which way the wind was blowing, he had volunteered for a major part in the enterprise and even offered to take personal command of the Office for Chastisement. The eventual plan, set in motion just after the New Year of 1281, called for some 50,000 Mongol, Korean, and North China soldiers to embark in Korean ships and meet with another fleet from the south carrying 100,000 more Chinese off the island of Iki. The two fleets would then make a series of landings at strategic points along the Kyushu coast.

The Korean fleet was ready to put to sea early in the spring but the larger Chinese contingent needed more time to get ready and it was already late June when the rendezvous took place. This time landings were effected at several points along the coast, with an especially strong force assigned to the Shiga Peninsula. However, while the invaders were able to maintain their beachheads at Shiga and elsewhere, they did not succeed in turning or even in breaching the Japanese defense line. The desperate fighting along the coast went on from June 23, when the first landings were made, until mid-August when, once more, the weather came to Japan's rescue, this time even more dramatically than it had done seven years before.

August is the start of the typhoon season in southern Japan, and the invaders had every reason to expect the arrival of at least one of the great storms that customarily precede the autumn equinox. Now, however, the Mongol commanders—no doubt smarting from the recollection of what had happened in 1274—chose to ignore whatever warnings their sea captains had the temerity to offer. Thus, when a major typhoon—to be known to Japanese history ever afterward as the *kamikaze,* or "wind from Heaven"—struck on the afternoon of August 15, the invaders were caught in precisely the grim predicament which had been foretold in comparable circumstances seven years earlier.

This time a few of the Korean captains, whose ships were for the most part at the northern end of the line, managed to get their soldiers aboard the vessels before the storm reached its height, but most of these foundered after reaching the open sea. In the south, where the full force of the wind smashed into the Chinese fleet crowded into the Gulf of Imari on northwest Kyushu, the effects were even more disastrous. Most of the soldiers who managed to embark were drowned when the vessels collided and sank while trying to clear the narrow neck of the harbor. Of the ships that did reach the sea, many were subsequently blown onto the rocks. The thousands of soldiers left on shore became prisoners and later slaves. While no reliable figures are available, no more than a small remnant of the gigantic armada ever regained the mainland.

In the years that followed, the possibility of a third Mongol invasion remained a threat—and one which was to have noteworthy political and economic effects inside Japan. In fact, however, Kublai Khan was having enough trouble on other segments of his vast imperial perimeter to prevent his giving serious consideration to another overseas assault. After his death in 1294, the danger gradually dwindled to the vanishing point, and from August 16, 1281, until the Japanese surrender on August 15, 1945, no invader ever again set foot on the Japanese islands —for whose inhabitants the manner in which the repulse of the Mongol effort had been accomplished provided fresh confirmation of their own divine origins.

The conclusion of the Mongol threat also had another less predictable but more immediate effect on political developments inside Japan. When the bakufu had first been set up in Kamakura, it was essentially a sort of family government cemented together by long-standing kinships and clan loyalties that had been tested and tightened during the wars between the Taira and the Minamoto. That the Hojo regents were themselves a branch of the Taira helped heal the scars of the bitter blood feuds from which the shogunate evolved. Nonetheless, the economic foundation of the Kamakura regime—which consisted primarily of the right to assign important administrative jobs and lucrative domains to deserving relatives—had at least one inherent and incurable defect. Since such jobs were hereditary and since the holders usually had more than one son, there had grown up over the years a vast number of offspring whose fractional shares of the paternal estates produced revenues well below the subsistence level.

Under the immediate threat of Mongol invasion, national unity had naturally taken priority over selfish motivations, but as the threat subsided unrest among Hojo and Minamoto relatives and vassals reappeared in considerably exacerbated form. Now, in addition to swarms of cadet kinsmen whose needs had been more or less ignored during thirty years of emergency, there were the captains and chiefs who felt that their services in manning the coast-line forts or in fighting on the beaches deserved special and prompt reward. After the war with the Taira, the forfeited lands of the losers had been available as prizes for the victors, but the repulse of the Mongol invaders, achieved at much greater cost, had brought no spoils whatever. The bitterness and discontent which followed the victory, and which the passage of time only served to intensify, came to a head early in the fourteenth century with the attempt on the part of an unruly Kyoto emperor named Go-Daigo, or Daigo II, to improve the situation by reasserting the imperial power.

When a majority of the warriors of western Japan—those who had been as a group the most active in repelling the invasion and the least favored by the Kamakura bakufu—joined forces with Go-Daigo, the bakufu sent its ablest general, Ashikaga Takauji, to subdue the revolt. Instead, with a flexibility of conviction which was thereafter to prove a salient feature of his character, Takauji became the emperor's ally. When the Hojo summoned another western chieftain to arms, he heeded the call only insofar as to join forces with Takauji and Go-Daigo in a campaign that led to the total downfall of the bakufu in 1334. Last of the Hojo regents was Takahito, an eccentric animal fancier who kept five thousand dogs, some of whom had their own palanquins. He and seven hundred of his followers committed suicide, leaving the dogs to shift for themselves.

The reign of the Kamakura bakufu had lasted for almost a hundred and fifty years, but that of Go-Daigo lasted for less than five. When he failed to show his gratitude to Takauji by handing over the reins of power, Takauji had him ejected from Kyoto, placed a scion of a collateral branch of the imperial line on the throne, and set himself up as

A guardian figure scowls menacingly from his post at Horyuji Temple, Nara.

shogun, with headquarters in Kyoto's Muromachi district from which the ensuing period of Japan's history takes its name. The dispute between the rival lines of the royal house was to continue for more than half a century. Meanwhile, the general's own Ashikaga clan established in 1338 a new bakufu that would last for the next two hundred and fifty years, during which, with no outside threats to worry about, Japan's denizens devoted themselves to a variety of domestic pursuits which, while multiple civil war took top priority, included commerce, the fine arts, and, perhaps most notably, affairs of the spirit.

In considering Buddhism, which is usually described as one of the four great religions of the world along with Judeo-Christianity, Islam, and Hinduism, one point to bear in mind is that unlike these it lacks the ingredient of God. As originally promulgated, the best it offered in the way of personal afterlife was a condition of blessed peace and forgetfulness called Nirvana. What Buddhism did have to offer instead of post-mortem benefits, however, was an admirable eight-paragraph prescription for the good life on earth as devised by its founder, Prince Gautama, to whom the birth date usually assigned is 563 B.C.

In the course of centuries of transmutation, the teachings of Gautama have been so elaborately expanded, interpreted, and codified in different lands and at different times that their relationship to his original Eightfold Path often seems distinctly remote. In Japan, where the first report on the subject arrived a thousand years later, these elaborations were eventually carried to a characteristic extreme. The tenets of one sect, for example, seem so similar to the teachings of Jesus Christ that students may be moved to wonder whether some New Testament precepts may not also derive from grapevine communication from India in the opposite direction.

To trace the history of Buddhism from its original sources to its flowering in such Japanese sects as Zen, Nichiren, or Jodo would require vast erudition and numerous volumes. These volumes have already been written and the subject may therefore be dealt with here in suitably truncated style. What seems to have occurred is that Buddhism, after its acceptance in principle as part of the Great Reform of 645, seeped down from the royal court to the common people—rather slowly at first but more rapidly as the spread of literacy made it possible for the latter to read its scriptures. Some of the mutations which were thereafter introduced into the doctrine are especially noteworthy for the light they reflect on the creative states of mind that produced them.

According to original Buddhist doctrine, what happens to each individual after death depends largely on his or her "karma," a sort of lifetime report card on deportment. Bad karma results in another life on a lower plane; top-notch karma results in enlightenment and promotion to the status of Buddhahood. In the sleepy lands of the south, this might be equated with Nirvana, but the interpretation favored by the mercurial Japanese was one which more closely resembled the Christian concept of Paradise. One of the earlier mortals to attain Buddhahood was a renowned disciple named Amida who demonstrated his enlightenment by stating that he would only accept such elevation on condition that other mortals could be similarly exalted if they expressed a sincere faith in him and in his principles.

More to the point than the similarity in some respects of Amida's teachings to those of Christ may be that, in any case, the notion that faith as well as good works constitutes an acceptable passport to Heaven made just as rapid progress in Japan as it had when promulgated in Judea. The ritual of "Nembutsu"—that is, the murmuring of the phrase *"Namu Amida Butsu"* meaning "Homage to Amida Buddha"—was presently further popularized by the teachings of one of Amida's disciples, to the effect that the formula could and should be used not only for the benefit of the worshiper, but also—as it had been by Amida himself—for that of all other mortals. Recital of the Nembutsu formula became as universal in the temples of Japan as recitals of the rosary in the churches of Europe. One emperor who, like many others of the Heian period spent his retirement years in a cloister, was said to have repeated the formula several millions of times and was still reciting it when he finally expired.

The elevation of Buddhist doctrine from the area of ethics and philosophy to that of celestial metaphysics and its extension into numerous subsidiary credos and conventions was, like the worship of Amida, by no means confined to Japan. Nonetheless, once it got there from the mainland, where there were more competing faiths, it proliferated with typical Japanese celerity and vigor. One outgrowth of the worship of

Amida was the so-called Jodo, or "Pure Land," sect which was opportunely launched by a monk named Honen in 1175, just when Pure Land, that is, Paradise, was a matter of primary concern to the large segment of the population involved in the hazardous struggle between the Taira and the Minamoto. An outgrowth of the Pure Land sect was the Ikko, or "True Pure Land" sect, which survives as an active force in Japan even today. Launched by Honen's disciple, Shinran, it was a further popularization of its parent faith.

Devotees of the True Pure Land sect stressed "equality for all in Buddhism," minimized the distinction between monks and laymen, and emphasized discussion groups. These, like other Buddhist organizations, often became leagues or congregations whose monastic centers acquired substantial political influence and power. During the fifteenth century, a True Pure Land sect coalition in western Japan ousted the feudal constables of two provinces and thereafter governed the area themselves. A century later the sect's great Honganji, or castle-cathedral, around which the city of Osaka grew up, became a major military stronghold. It defied Nobunaga, the greatest feudal captain of the era, in a siege that lasted for ten years.

Even more closely akin to Christianity than the Ikko and Jodo sects—in its concern with the afterlife on the one hand and its militant proselytizing on the other—was a third popular Buddhist movement named after its founder, a monk called Nichiren. Unlike Honen, Shinran, and other renowned priests who respected the fundamentally peaceful traditions of Buddhism in dealing with each other, Nichiren was an angry and outspoken sage who considered all forms of Buddhism other than his own as anathema and made no secret of his views, which represent a foretaste, if not foundation, of later Japanese nationalism.

While Nichiren, Ikko, and Jodo were in essence popular movements, the form of Buddhism that appealed most to the warriors, aristocrats, and rulers of the Ashikaga era was one which has more recently been given a worldwide welcome by contemporary hippies and dropouts—most of whom are perhaps happily unaware of its origins. Brought to Japan from China by the student-monks who accompanied the first embassies to Ch'ang-an, Zen Buddhism combined elements of both Confucian philosophy and Chinese mysticism with reverence for Gau-

A screen shows the Amida Buddha in the Western Paradise with his attendants. Such painted screens were placed before the dying as a source of comfort.

tama. In Japan its most influential exponent was a monk who elucidated its principles first to Go-Daigo and then to Takauji—to whom
he shrewdly transferred his loyalties after the demotion of his former
imperial patron.

Enough has been said in recent years about the wisdom of Zen teachings and the occult significance of such questions as what kind of a
noise results when one claps with only one hand, as to make it apparent that the values which this doctrine has to offer its initiates are often
so subtle as to escape the ordinary Occidental reader. However, certain
essential elements of Zen teachings underlie much Japanese thought
and behavior and should be briefly enumerated. These include emphasis on meditation as a basis for action, on strength of character and self-
reliance, and on the integration of mind and muscle, as perhaps over-
simplified most lucidly for Westerners in the Roman concept of *mens
sana in corpore sano*. Under the Ashikaga shoguns, the great Nan-
zenji monastery in Kyoto became the official presiding Zen institution,
and its abbot, if not a Japanese pope, was at least the nation's closest
equivalent to an archbishop of Canterbury.

Because the militarism of the Kamakura period in Japanese history
contrasted so sharply with the elegance of the preceding Heian era
there is a tendency to suppose that under the Hojo regents Japan as a
whole experienced a total cultural black-out. Actually, this is in some
respects the reverse of what occurred. Because the Kamakura warriors
disliked being regarded as rustic louts by their cultural seniors in the
east, they hastened to take a cram course in civilized traditions so as
to acquire at least a veneer of Chinese sophistication. Kamakura's
world-renowned Daibutsu (Great Buddha)—a heroic bust of Amida
cast in 1252 and still reputed to be the largest bronze statue in the
world—was the most spectacular physical evidence of this spiritual
growth but by no means the only one.

During the 150 years when Kamakura was the capital, artists, writers, and learned monks congregated there as they had previously done
at Kyoto, with the result that the erudition which had previously been
concentrated in the imperial court achieved some degree of general
dissemination. One reason that the Minamoto had been so ready to set
up their unpretentious headquarters on the east coast and style it a
mere bakufu may have been precisely because they felt ill at ease amid

the refinements of metropolitan Kyoto. Conversely, one reason that the Ashikaga were ready to go back to the old capital and settle down in its Muromachi district in 1392 may have been that by this time the cultural disparity between the two regions had perceptibly diminished.

By the same token, because Japan's two and a half centuries under the Ashikaga—known to historians as the Muromachi period—were largely characterized by political strife and internal commotion, there is a tendency to suppose that this period also failed in every respect to compare culturally to the Heian golden age. The reality again was rather that under the Ashikaga, Japan's cultural development, while less rapid and concentrated, became more generalized and diffuse. While religion, literature, and the arts were often overshadowed in public attention by civil dissension, interest in them continued to proliferate despite interruptions; and where the removal of the invasion threat provided the opportunity for further growth, a new impetus was provided by the teachings of the great Zen monasteries. Under the aegis of the central institution at Kyoto, these spread their enlightenment throughout the rugged and mountainous countryside, especially to the communities between Kyoto and the by then equally populous and thriving area in and around the Kanto plain.

Among Japanese literary developments under the Ashikaga rulers, the most striking novelty was the *Noh* plays which, rather like the miracle plays from which the Elizabethan drama gradually evolved, were originally teaching aids devised by monk-dramatists in order to inculcate religious concepts as effectively as possible. However, while the Noh drama, with its stylized gestures and medieval masks, remains alive and flourishing today in somewhat the same way as Shakespearean drama in English-speaking countries, this was by no means the only or even the main avenue of artistic advance opened up under the new regime in Kyoto. Even more noteworthy was progress in the fine arts of architecture and painting.

Despite the tendency of their buildings, especially the larger ones, to fall down or burn up during earthquakes, Japanese architects were nonetheless encouraged to do magnificent work as early as the Nara period. This, according to the United States Gothic specialist Ralph Adams Cram, had produced "the most precious architecture in all Asia" in the form of the double-roofed Golden Hall of the Horyuji

Monastery dating back to A.D. 607. Despite perennial renovations of minor elements, this is still usually considered the oldest wooden building now standing in the world. Comparable masterpieces of the Muromachi period are the country villas of two early Ashikaga shoguns near Kyoto, known as the Kinkaku, or Golden Pavilion, and the Ginkaku, or Silver Pavilion. Built in 1394 and 1479 respectively, these exemplify to perfection the Japanese genius for integrating any structure with its surroundings in ways that were to influence Western taste only several hundred years later.

That Westerners took so long to appreciate—and to try to adapt to their own Occidental forms—such harmonious accord between buildings and background is perhaps not altogether surprising, since its very purpose is to escape, rather than to attract, attention. As such it embodies one aspect of the Zen principle that "great mastery is as if unskillful," which, if it did not predate the Latin principle that art is to conceal art, certainly anticipates Mies van der Rohe's "less is more." What prompted the definition was a painting by Josetsu, an early Muromachi master who helped make new trends in painting perhaps the period's most notable contribution to the whole field of aesthetics. Zen emphasis on nature as subject matter and on spontaneity in treatment led to a deceptively offhand style of black and white landscape painting in pure ink, or *sumi,* characterized by powerful brush strokes, bold ink washes, and the elimination of nonessential detail. While it owed much to the work of contemporary artists in China, this style reached its epitome in Japan under Josetsu, his disciples Shubun and Sesshu, and later the painters of the Kano school, named after its founders, Kano Masanobu and his son, Motonobu. Direct descendants of the Kano family, which is unique in the whole history of art for the durability of its influence, were to dominate Japanese painting until well into the nineteenth century.

When Japanese artists adapt or expand techniques that have been originated elsewhere, they are liable to the familiar charge by Western critics of being mere copyists. However, when they originate new fields of their own, the same critics are often equally apt to belittle, if not to dismiss, their creations for not being within what Europeans regard as the boundaries of the fine arts. Three examples of this artistic eclecticism that developed during the Muromachi period were landscape gardening, flower arranging, and the tea ceremony. While all three owe much to Chinese practices that preceded their introduction to Japan, it was in Japan that they attained the lofty aesthetic status which they still enjoy there.

The tea ceremony apparently owed its first popularity to Ashikaga Yoshimasa, the owner of the Ginkaku, who took it up on the advice of his friend, the painter Noami. The latter had written him a letter on the subject starting "There is a thing called tea ceremony . . ." and going on to explain that a monk named Shuko had devoted thirty years to studying it. To define the tea ceremony as a fine art may be doing it an injustice since it utilizes elements of several arts in creating what is sometimes described as a religious experience. Partly as a means of attaining the serenity and relaxation appropriate to Zen meditation, participants in this ceremony start by inspecting and admiring the bowl in which the tea is served—usually an old and deceptively unpretentious one. The tea, in powdered form, is then mixed by the host and tasted by each guest in turn. A quiet conversation takes place after which the guests disperse. For the European novice unaccustomed to sitting cross-legged on a straw mat and incapable of judging the merits of the tea, the tea bowl, or a Japanese conversation conducted along Zen lines, the whole program is inevitably a test of physical endurance rather than of spiritual sensibility, but this hardly invalidates its potential significance for more competent participants.

Japanese landscape gardening and flower arrangement are related media which also reflect Zen emphasis on nature in its quieter manifestations and in which again the merit of the medium lies in using art to conceal art. Flower gardens like those admired in Western countries are nonexistent in Japan; such wholesale displays of bloom would be at once too ostentatious and too artificial for a taste which runs to a few choice stones and a trickle of water dripping through an enclave of trees, plants, and moss-covered earth. Flowers are to be cut elsewhere and employed indoors to serve somewhat the same purpose as that for which modern Europeans employ the more primitive device of a fireplace, to give color, life, and focus to a room.

In Japan arranging flowers (*ikebana*) is not a casual knack to be picked up in a few minutes by anyone with a sharp eye for shape and color. It is a creative form with complex rules and principles, some rudiments of which have been a part of every well-brought-up Japanese girl's education since the fifteenth century. Good flower arrangements should, and often do, display the spontaneity and compositional impact of first-rate abstract painting with the distinction that, instead of being hung up as permanent wall fixtures which presently grow tiresome, they can be tossed out and replaced by fresh ones the next week.

Along with the arts, and to some extent as a result of them, another line of endeavor that flourished during the politically distraught Muromachi era was commerce with the mainland. Now prospering under the Ming dynasty which had succeeded the Mongol khans, China was once more a source not only of intellectual and aesthetic inspiration but also of tangible commodities such as silk, tea, porcelain, and copper coins. In return, Japan exported such varied raw materials as timber, gold, and natural pearls along with such products of her skilled artisans as folding fans, painted screens, and samurai swords.

In earlier days, much of the commerce between China and Japan—which had been going on to some extent ever since the first embassies—had been carried by Korean ships, but during the fourteenth century Japanese junks began to assume a larger share of the burden. By the end of the fifteenth, they dominated the greatly increased coastwide traffic, some of which was financed by the great monastic orders and some even by the Ashikaga themselves. Even more was encouraged or conducted by certain major landowning clans, especially the Shimazu of Kyushu whose family flag, the sun on a white background, presently became accepted in foreign ports as that of the Japanese nation. Adventurous Japanese traders settled down in the harbor towns of southern China, Malaya, the Philippines, and even Siam. In the sixteenth century their paths began to cross those of Portuguese mariners whose ships were beginning to reach the same ports via the Cape of Good Hope.

Along with commerce went piracy, which during the sixteenth century ravaged the entire Chinese coast to such an extent that the Ming rulers, in vain hopes of stopping it, decreed an end to Chinese shipping and even to shipbuilding. The result of this ill-considered ban was to force numerous Chinese sailors theretofore engaged in legitimate trade to become pirates; quite frequently, in order to avoid detection, they took the guise of Japanese, since Japanese *wako,* or freebooters, some of whom were pirates and some merely adventurers trading without government license, did indeed account for a substantial share of the problem.

Some indication of the complexities involved in dealing with piracy was provided by the case of one enterprising Chinese pirate chief named Wang Chih who moved to Japan in 1545 and invited Japanese merchants to join him in large-scale smuggling operations whereby Japanese goods would be bartered for Chinese at a secret rendezvous in the islands off the South China coast. The arrangement worked admirably and Wang Chih prospered until the Chinese government sent a mission to Japan to ask the bakufu for help in putting a stop to piracy in general. Wang Chih obligingly explained to these emissaries that the bakufu was quite powerless to do anything of the sort but that he himself, if pardoned by the Ming government for previous offenses, might be able to help out by dealing directly with the *daimyo,* or feudal barons, under whose protection the pirates operated. The envoys agreed but when Wang Chih returned to China he was promptly executed. Piracy on the high seas continued to flourish as vigorously as terrestrial strife among the war lords on the Japanese islands.

By the time the Ashikaga shoguns appeared on the scene, the main island of Honshu had been fairly well cleared of the distasteful Ainu, and the nation as a whole was subdivided into some sixty provinces corresponding more or less to those in evidence today. The political order differed chiefly from that which had preceded it under the Hojo regents in that the centralized power which had then been concentrated in the bakufu was now dispersed among the hereditary daimyo. While the degree of local autonomy exercised by such overlords varied from place to place, most of the provinces were already, or presently became, small principalities which fought their private wars and made their private alliances with little or no interference from the shoguns. As the latter became increasingly less concerned with exerting military power than with enjoying the amenities of life in the capital, further developments occurred. Just as the Fujiwara family had manipulated the Kamakura shoguns, a new family called the Hosokawa appeared on the scene to handle the tiresome chores of

state business on behalf of the Ashikaga. And now, with the chief function of the emperor as a sort of *arbiter elegantiae* usurped by the shogun, and with the function of the Fujiwara usurped by the Hoso-kawa, the old court families and even the emperor himself fell on times which were to test the stamina of the latter's divinity to the utmost.

Mainly dependent on the bakufu for revenue, the Muromachi-period emperors found themselves often not only relegated to the background socially but too short of cash to meet the day-to-day expenses of maintaining their dwindling court. One descendant of the Sun Goddess, when he died in 1500, remained unburied for six weeks because the treasury lacked funds for his funeral. His successor's cor-onation was delayed twenty years for the same reason. Another un-fortunate denizen of the imperial palace was reduced to peddling his

Zen Buddhism emphasizes contemplation and communion with nature whether it be in a wooded grove or the more abstract setting of an artfully raked garden.

calligraphy on the street outside it. When requested to do so, he would dash off a line or two of classic verse, adding the royal cypher to complete the composition.

Among the minor arts that flourished under the Ashikaga shoguns, one was naturally that of writing histories wherein the squabbles among the great landowning clans were covered down to the last bowl of rice consumed by their hungry samurai. Such chronicles make fascinating reading, for it was an era of vast turmoil and mobility in which great nobles lost their estates or their lives and poor adventurers became millionaires or great nobles, all with a suitable accompaniment of heroism, treachery, murder, rape, and other evidences of lively human commotion.

After inspecting one historic battleground, the poet Matsuo Basho, looking backward from the seventeenth century, offered a pertinent comment:

The summer grasses!
All that is left of the warrior's dream!

Owing partly to the isolated situation of Japan and partly to the vigorous growth of summer grasses everywhere else in the world, the discernible impact of all these gory goings on upon the history of mankind was not much greater than if they had taken place on some undiscovered planet—except, of course, for the descendants of the warriors involved. Since such descendants compose a large portion of contemporary Japanese TV and movie audiences, feudal battles are re-enacted on their screens as often as the doings of the North American Wild West upon screens elsewhere.

One question that may arise is why, if the decline in power of the Heian court led to the decisive war between the Taira and the Minamoto, did not the eventual decline in power of the Ashikaga produce some similar showdown and some comparable recentralization of power? Actually, a showdown did eventually occur; but, perhaps because the factions were now so much more numerous and the competition consequently much keener, the process took considerably longer. During the latter half of the fourteenth century, the dispute between the two imperial lines was finally settled by the forced abdication of

Go-Daigo in favor of the junior line installed by Takauji. Thereafter civil dissension took the form chiefly of local disturbances which the Ashikaga shoguns managed to survive albeit with diminished authority.

In 1467 a peculiarly venomous civil war broke out which lasted for a decade and resulted in the passing of the residual shogunate power from the Ashikaga to the Hosokawa family. The latter, however, instead of claiming the shogunate for themselves, preferred to use the title of *kanrei,* or deputy shogun, and to rule through a line of puppet Ashikaga with names like Yoshitane, Yoshizumi, Yoshiharu, Yoshiteru, Yoshihide, and Yoshiaki. Thus, after a century or so of localized but incessant civil war, the country was split up among a score or so of leading daimyo and long overdue for a reunification which finally took place in three stages during the late sixteenth and early seventeenth centuries.

The first stage of the reunification occurred under the leadership of Oda Nobunaga, previously mentioned as the warrior who subdued the True Pure Land sect castle at Osaka. As the off-shoot of an old daimyo family whose hereditary fiefdom comprised some three provinces to the east of Kyoto, Nobunaga first made himself master of these as a base for further operations which presently gave him control of the capital and later of some twenty other provinces previously controlled by rival daimyo or by the great monasteries. However, in 1582, before Nobunaga could finish consolidating the rest of the country, he died at the hands of a treacherous subordinate in 1582, whereupon command of his armies passed to his top general, Toyotomi Hideyoshi.

One of the most colorful figures in the whole bright pageant of Japanese history, the brainy, ambitious, and indefatigable Hideyoshi was a peasant's son of such humble origins that he lacked even a last name until the emperor conferred one on him as a reward for services. Having started out in life as a bandit, he had clawed his way up the military ladder by courage, effrontery, and sheer good luck. Within three years after the death of his chief, he had brought Japan so completely under his control that he felt ready for further conquest. Partly to keep his armies busy and partly perhaps because he sensed that such a venture would further consolidate his rule, he announced to the emperor that his next move would be to annex China, which he proposed to invade via Korea. "I shall do it," he explained, "as easily as a man picks up a piece of straw matting and carries it away under his arm."

In fact, though Hideyoshi's expeditionary forces did overrun Korea, they suffered a serious setback, like those of Douglas MacArthur a few centuries later, when Chinese armies crossed the Yalu to stop them. Nonetheless, the fact that Japan had now become powerful enough not merely to repulse an invasion from the mainland but to reverse the process in a fashion untried since the days of Queen Jingo, was a clue to the new interior cohesion that had abruptly replaced the anarchic divisions of the previous two and a half centuries. Instead of the title of shogun, which he perhaps felt required a more exalted family background than he could bring to it, Hideyoshi preferred to style himself *taiko,* or tycoon, the appellation usually used by an imperial regent on retiring from office. As such, while his armies in Korea held to a defensive foothold around Pusan, Hideyoshi had several years of relative leisure in which, with the aid of some three hundred concubines, to enjoy nationwide adulation until his death in 1598.

On Hideyoshi's demise, command passed to his deputy, Tokugawa Ieyasu, who had been running the eastern section of the now reunified realm from the small village of Edo, a few miles north of Kamakura. Before the death of his chief, Ieyasu had promised to see that the

Swords such as these were part of the armor of the fierce samurai *class.*

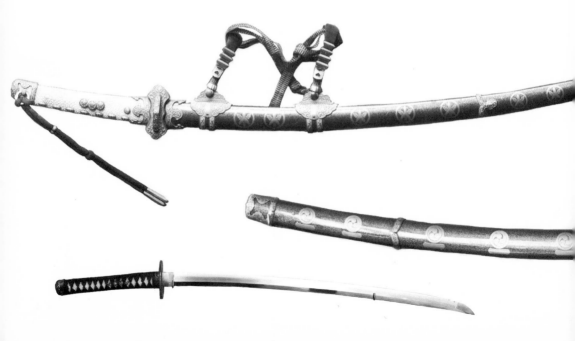

regency of Japan eventually passed to Hideyoshi's infant son, Hideyori. However, before arranging this, he felt himself obliged to eliminate all other possible rivals. Doing so required fifteen years and involved appropriating some of their former properties himself and redistributing the remainder to his own adherents. By the time he had accomplished this, a substantial swarm of dispossessed daimyo and their followers had joined Hideyori, hoping that he would help redress their grievances. Ieyasu laid siege to Hideyori's Osaka citadel, whose occupant avoided eventual capture only by committing suicide. Then, having exterminated all of the latter's male offspring, legitimate and otherwise, Ieyasu turned to the major task of finding a way to ensure the permanence and stability of his own regime.

On his death a few years later, Ieyasu's will was found to contain a revealing, if somewhat sanctimonious, statement of his guiding principles. It ran as follows:

"Life is like unto a long journey with a heavy burden. Let thy step be slow and steady, that thou stumble not. Persuade thyself that imperfection and inconvenience is the natural lot of mortals, and there will be no room for discontent, neither for despair. When ambitious desires arise in thy heart, recall the days of extremity thou has passed through. Forbearance is the root of quietness and assurance forever. Look upon wrath as thy enemy. If thou knowest only what

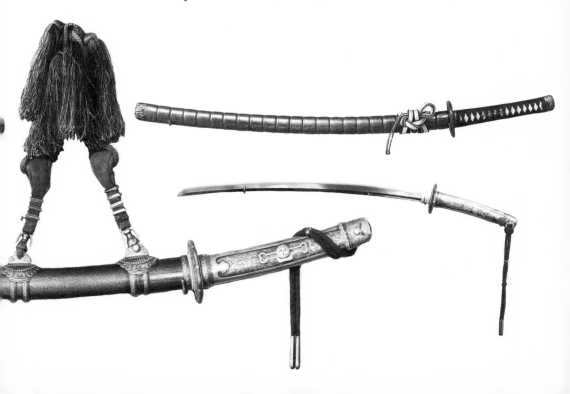

it is to conquer, and knowest not what it is to be defeated, woe unto thee; it will fare ill with thee. Find fault with thyself rather than with others."

Unlike his ebullient predecessor, the author of this document had no appetite for ventures like the invasion of Korea, which he suspended soon after Hideyoshi's death. Instead, Ieyasu saw, perhaps more clearly than anyone since Yoritomo five centuries earlier, that Japan's real problem was not how to win new territory on the mainland but how to administer that already in hand. The origins of Japan's domestic problem were, first, the nature of the terrain, which made communications and hence a chain of authority so difficult to establish; and second, the fierce vitality of the inhabitants which, when not firmly yoked to some sensible objective, would expend itself in introverted competition all the more furious for being essentially futile. What was needed was not merely the prudent exercise of power during his lifetime but an arrangement whereby such power could be handed on to his heirs without further struggles like those he himself had just experienced in attaining it.

To satisfy these two objectives, Ieyasu started by having himself declared shogun and establishing his capital at Edo where the splendid fortifications of his castle were to constitute the heart of what, under its subsequent name of Tokyo, would become the world's largest city. The bakufu which he established there was not a mere makeshift affair dependent on clan loyalties and marital kinships. It was a carefully devised organization under which the nation was divided into three regions, each with certain well-defined obligations and responsibilities. First came the home provinces between Edo and Kyoto, where three cadet branches of the Tokugawa family were to hold sway from three major centers. Second came the surrounding regions, whose ruling *fudai,* or hereditary daimyo, had supported Ieyasu throughout his efforts to gain unquestioned authority. Finally came the more remote regions to the north, south, and west, most of which had only acknowledged his supremacy late in the day and which would be ruled by *tozama,* or "outer daimyo."

All daimyo, though they would be allowed a relatively free hand in their own domains, would be expected to show complete fealty to the shogun at Edo. To make sure that none of them got any false ideas about who was running the country, each would spend part of the year in Edo and leave some members of his family there when he went back to his fiefdom for the other part. And to make sure that everyone knew who was going to succeed to the shogunate and that the succession went off smoothly, Ieyasu retired and handed the title on to his son who took office two years before his father's death in 1616.

In the years to come, Ieyasu's successors completed the establishment of a bakufu along far more advanced lines than either its early prototype in Kamakura or its immediate predecessor in Kyoto. At its head was a prime minister and a council of elders, mostly drawn from the ample ranks of the Tokugawa family. Beneath these was an important group of officials called *metsuke*—actually a sort of intelligence agency whose job was to report instances of maladministration on the one hand or evidence of subversive intrigue on the other. Beneath the bakufu, society was rigidly divided, along more or less Confucian lines, into four classes: first, the ruling daimyo and their samurai adherents; second, peasants and farmers who represented 80 per cent of the population; third, artisans; and lowest of all, the merchants.

This is what in modern times could justifiably be described as a police state with the emperor at Kyoto occupying more or less the role of a constitutional monarch. In many respects, the whole system sounds hopelessly impractical, but in fact it worked reasonably well. Under the Tokugawa shoguns, Japan enjoyed for the next 250 years internal harmony as complete as had been the confusion of the 250 preceding ones. When the Tokugawa shogunate finally fell in the latter half of the nineteenth century, it was due less to interior causes than to totally unforeseen happenings elsewhere.

CHAPTER IV

BAKUFU VS. OLD BRUIN

From the year 1600, when Tokugawa Ieyasu dispersed his main rivals at the Battle of Sekigahara, until 1867 when the last of his descendants was to abdicate at Edo, the Tokugawa shogunate covered roughly the same span of time as that in which England acquired a world-wide empire. Triggered by victory over the Spanish Armada, the bold performance of the British, as the vanguard of the westward-faring segment of mankind, was in marked contrast to the behavior of its counterpart in the Far East. What Japan's thirteenth-century victory over the Mongols—comparable on some counts to Britain's over Spain —had triggered was two and a half centuries of furious internal squabbling under the Ashikaga. Now, given two and a half centuries of internal tranquility under their Tokugawa successors, the Japanese devoted them to total seclusion from the rest of the world. The cause of this unique display of national introversion—quite as spectacular in its way as the simultaneous display of extraversion by Great Britain —deserves investigation.

The immediate occasion for Japan's abrupt and complete withdrawal from the rest of the world—like that of her equally abrupt

The tea ceremony, still performed today, was an important ritual in court life.

emergence two and a half centuries later—was not the consequence of a whim on the part of an eccentric shogun. It was an understandable response to the pressure of exterior forces. During the sixteenth century, while Spain was heading west to develop an empire in the Americas, Portugal was heading east to do likewise in Africa and Asia. The Ming dynasty's edict against shipbuilding by the Chinese—who might otherwise have chased the newcomers out of the Indian Ocean —gave Portugal, with bases already established at Goa and Malacca, a free hand along the South China coast. The result was a settlement at Macao—nowadays still much in evidence—through which to trade with the Chinese at nearby Canton. In due course, a coasting junk, in which three Portuguese businessmen had booked passage, was blown off course by a typhoon. The junk put in at the island of Tanegashima, off the Kyushu coast, where the inhabitants were understandably impressed by the contents of the foreigners' sample cases. The most conspicuous items were firearms.

A year or two later, when Portuguese trading ships began to appear along the coast of Kyushu, the resident daimyo, having already heard about the guns, were naturally receptive. Thereafter, Portuguese visitors were welcomed in Japanese ports, and "Tanegashima weapons," first imported and later of domestic manufacture, became a familiar fixture of domestic battlefields—where, however, they were to remain less popular than the sword. Along with the traders on the Portuguese ships came Jesuit missionaries; the Kyushu daimyo, observing the deference which the clerics were accorded by the captains and crews of their vessels, treated them with similar respect.

One of the first and certainly one of the most effective missionaries to Japan was a well-born young priest named Francis Xavier who, a few years before his arrival, had helped Ignatius Loyola found the Jesuit order. Father Xavier landed at Kagoshima in 1549 and spent the next two years learning the language, traveling about the country on foot, and making numerous converts whose eager response and subsequent devotion he found deeply moving. On his departure for Goa, he took with him a Japanese mission whose members presently returned to continue his work. Father Xavier's death, on his way to China the following year, fortunately occurred far too soon for him to learn the tragic results of his labors in Japan which, indeed, would only become fully apparent some years after his canonization in 1622.

For the warm reception which Christianity received from the Japanese many reasons have been advanced. One is that Kyushu, where it got its start, is a harsh and infertile region whose peasants, with an even harder lot to bear than those on the islands to the north, were especially responsive to the message of hope provided by the Gospels. Another is that the daimyo in the western provinces had noticed that profitable trade tended to follow the missionaries and deduced that encouraging them might be the most effective means of attracting the merchant vessels. A third reason may possibly have been that, along with its ingratiating theories about posthumous resurrection, Christian doctrine presented in the Trinity a pantheon of which the organization chart somewhat resembled the familiar one of emperor, shogun, and regent. In any case, the new faith made rapid headway. By 1580 there were an estimated 150,000 Japanese Christians, mostly in and about Nagasaki where Portuguese ships usually anchored, and by the end of the century a good many thousands more.

While most of the converts were poor peasants or farmers, the fact that some of these were influenced to join the Church by their superiors was proof that the new movement also attracted a surprisingly large share of the aristocracy. In addition to the trade-conscious Kyushu daimyo, Christianity had great appeal for women, especially ladies of the court; by the 1590s, converts included the closest friend of Hideyoshi's wife and the sister of one of his favorite mistresses. In 1582 the three leading Christian daimyo of Kyushu sent several patrician youths on a mission to Europe which they reached via Acapulco, Mexico. After visits to Portugal and Spain, they kissed the foot of Pope Gregory XIII and eventually returned home via the Cape of Good Hope after an absence of eight years.

Although the new faith was understandably viewed with marked disfavor by the powerful Buddhist sects, Japan's rulers during the period under which it made its initial rapid gains saw no reason to disparage it on that account. Nobunaga, amply engaged in feuding with True Pure Land Buddhists, paid little attention to the Christians; and his successor, Hideyoshi, seemed equally indulgent toward them during the first part of his reign. Then in 1587, after an evening spent in the company of a distinguished missionary on board a Portuguese ship in the port of Hakata, Hideyoshi suddenly issued an edict banning Christianity and ordering all missionaries—by this time numbering about 150—to leave the country within twenty days.

What prompted Hideyoshi's sudden change of heart was never fully explained. According to one version, not wholly implausible in view of his renowned sexual proclivities, he found that the new gospel impaired the compliance of the young girls of the locality. Another was that he had acted in a fit of drunken impetuosity brought on by guzzling a bottle of strong wine given him as a farewell present by his host. In any event, although from then on Christians were subject to intermittent persecution, the edict of banishment was never strictly enforced. At the time of Hideyoshi's death in 1598, there were still a hundred or so Portuguese priests in and about Nagasaki which their parishioners by that time controlled as effectively as the Ikko sect had previously controlled Osaka.

During the early stages of Tokugawa Ieyasu's consolidation of power, he was too busy dealing with military rivals to concern himself with such minor threats as the spread of Christianity but, as the Battle of Sekigahara receded into the background, the perspective changed. Among the "outer daimyo," whose loyalties remained the most suspect, the most powerful, and the most difficult to get at remained the Shimazu, who not only ruled Satsuma and two other provinces in southern Kyushu, but also possessed what amounted to a powerful private navy. If the Christian daimyo of Kyushu were to combine under Shimazu leadership with the Portuguese, whose formidable warships could then be used to bring in a well-armed European invasion force, the result might well be a serious threat to Ieyasu's whole regime.

At about the time when Ieyasu was considering this dire possibility, a new element was introduced into the situation by the arrival in 1584 of Spanish traders from the Philippines, where Spain had acquired Manila primarily as a way stop on the Pacific route to Mexico and Peru. They were followed by Dutch and British vessels which, like the Spanish ships, used the port of Hirado, on the northwest coast of Kyushu. Doctrinal bickerings between the Franciscan and Dominican monks who accompanied the Spaniards and the Jesuits who had come with the Portuguese made it clear to the bakufu that European Chris-

A lacquered picnic box and decorated porcelain jar and dish are examples of an aesthetic sensibility applied to even the smallest details of daily life.

tianity was by no means a monolithic structure. When the Protestants arrived, in most cases without any missionaries whatsoever, the arguments became even more bitter as the newcomers accused the Catholics of using religious penetration as a means of securing commercial advantage—to which the Catholics replied that their Protestant rivals used trade as a pretext for political intrusion.

From reports of what was taking place elsewhere in Asia, Ieyasu could readily infer that, in the latter dispute, there was some truth on both sides. Nonetheless, it seemed apparent that commercial dealings with the Protestants could at least be conducted with fewer extraneous commitments than with their rivals. Eager to continue trading, if this could be done with no strings attached, Ieyasu began to see a solution to his immediate dilemma. The result, in January, 1614, was a new edict banning Christianity throughout Japan—and this time one that was promptly and vigorously put into effect. Churches were destroyed, missionaries deported, and Japanese Christians sent into exile or tortured in an effort, usually unsuccessful, to force them to recant.

Under Ieyasu's successors, the persecution of Christians increased in extent and severity, reaching a climax of sorts in 1622 when thirty Christians were beheaded and twenty-five, including nine foreign priests, burned at the stake in the town of Miyako. An eyewitness account of what mission reports referred to as the Great Martyrdom was supplied by an English trader named Richard Cocks: "I saw fifty-five of them martyred at one time. . . . Among them were little children of five or six years, burned alive in the arms of their mothers, who cried 'Jesus, receive their souls!' There are many in prison who hourly await death, for very few return to their idolatry."

As things turned out, even the Great Martyrdom was only a prologue to the gory last act in the tragic drama set in motion by Saint Francis Xavier and his colleagues. In 1638, driven to despairing revolt by combined economic and religious oppression, some 37,000 Christian peasants holed up in a disused castle on the Shimabara Peninsula near Nagasaki and there, captained by a handful of samurai converts, held out for three months against some 100,000 government troops. When the castle finally fell, all but 105 of its inmates were reported to have been hunted down and killed.

Although a few hardy souls continued to hold mass and practice

Christian rituals in secrecy thereafter, this appalling massacre—easily the greatest, even allowing for some statistical exaggeration, since Roman times—effactually put a stop to Christianity in Japan. However, far from allaying Tokugawa fears as to the mischievous potential of European intruders in general, and of the missionaries in particular, the Shimabara Rebellion and its aftermath only served to intensify them. The Spanish traders along with the monks from Manila had been ejected in 1624. Now, suspecting the Portuguese of complicity in the rebellion, the bakufu turned them out also. The British, whose traders had been the last to arrive on the scene, had already departed of their own accord. This left only the Dutch, whose ships had aided the government armies in reducing the stronghold at Shimabara. Their reward for this somewhat shabby contribution to Japan's political and territorial integrity was perhaps a commensurate one. It consisted of permission to maintain thereafter a tiny trickle of trade consisting of not more than two ships a year. Carrying miscellaneous cargoes composed largely of knickknacks and books—excluding, however, all works of a religious character—these ships were permitted to anchor at the dreary little islet of Deshima in Nagasaki harbor where a few Dutchmen were also permitted to remain in permanent residence. While a limited trade with licensed ships also continued from China, this minuscule commerce with the Netherlands was to be Japan's only contact with the Western world for more than two centuries.

A corollary reason for the preference shown to the Dutch was perhaps that, even before this time, the Japanese had become indebted to them on another score. In 1600 a Dutch vessel which had suffered severe damage in a typhoon had arrived in Kyushu after a voyage through the Strait of Magellan carrying remnants of her crew which included a highly competent English navigator named Will Adams. Summoned to appear before the bakufu, Adams became a trusted adviser of Ieyasu and stayed on in a role somewhat analogous to that of Marco Polo at the court of Kublai Khan three centuries earlier. Adams' knowledge of shipbuilding was helpful to the already extremely active Japanese merchant marine just then enjoying a surge of prosperity comparable to the one it was to experience in the decades following World War II. Thriving outposts of Japanese traders had developed in all the major seaports along the Asia coast and on the adjacent islands, including a colony of five thousand or so in Manila alone. Bangkok was another major outpost.

In its eagerness, intensified by the Shimabara Rebellion, to avoid any further political or evangelical pollution from the West, the bakufu was not content merely to exclude European visitors. With characteristic emphasis, it went the whole distance by forbidding even Japanese who had then been overseas for five years or more to return to their homeland. Members of the overseas trading colonies who did sneak home and were thereafter discovered were to be summarily put to death as were those rare individuals who, after being allowed to return, later tried to escape.

To make sure that in future no Japanese could go abroad to be contaminated by foreigners, the bakufu further forbade the construction of any ships larger than fishing boats or small craft for carrying cargo between the Japanese islands. And finally, in 1639, when the Portuguese were still suspected of smuggling in priests and religious articles, the government decreed that no Portuguese vessel would be admitted to any Japanese port and that if any disobeyed this edict, the vessel itself would be destroyed and its crew and passengers executed. When, the next year, the Portuguese had the temerity to send a mission from Macao to protest this ban, fifty-seven of its members were ceremoniously beheaded and the remaining thirteen sent back to Macao to report on their fate. In future years, even shipwrecked sailors who had the misfortune to be cast up on the shores of Japan were sometimes subject to similar punishment—though in most instances they were merely packed off, as rudely and rapidly as possible, through the Dutch station at Deshima.

Prisoners on their isolated islands for the next two hundred years, Japanese elsewhere than Nagasaki rarely even caught sight of a foreign ship, and when they did it was only against a distant horizon. Since all ships look black when seen against the sky, this led future generations of Japanese to suppose that all foreign ships, unlike their own unpainted coasting craft, were actually this color. "Black Ships" became the generic term for them.

According to most modern students of such matters, Japan's abrupt retirement from the world—to some degree comparable with

A nineteenth-century print by Hiroshige shows a gentleman at a posting house.

Weary travelers meet along the Tokaido Road which ran from Edo to Kyoto.

that of her early emperors who had made a practice of entering Buddhist retreats and maintaining their courts in monastic seclusion—was a monumental mistake from the viewpoint of national interest. Such critics point to the great advances achieved by European civilization in the interim and to the failure of the Japanese to keep pace. In fact, as was later to be made only too clear, the Japanese, when they felt impelled to do so, had no difficulty whatsoever in catching up. One reason they could do it so readily was that present-day estimates of European progress between 1600 and 1850 may be something of an illusion created by the technological progress really made in the century that followed. Had Japan not ejected the foreigners, it might well have become a mere colony; by doing so, it completely achieved the main objective, which was to preserve its national identity. Far from submitting to European domination like every other nation in Asia—except, for rather special reasons, Siam—Japan remained, just as it had during the period when the Mongols were conquering most of the world, a unique bastion of independence. Moreover, in the two centuries that followed, the nation used this rare status to considerable advantage.

In order to get a clear picture of Japanese life during—or, for that matter, even before—the period of the Tokugawa shoguns, it may be helpful to have some clues as to the economic underpinnings. That Japan was then and is now able to feed twice as many people as England on the produce of less than half as much arable land is due primarily to the kind of food the land produces. Instead of devouring huge quantities of beef and dairy products, the Japanese subsist much more economically on rice; and while some modern dieticians take a poor view of such undeviating consumption of carbohydrates, the facts do not altogether support them. While smaller than most Europeans, the Japanese often seem much nimbler; they also exert about as many foot-pounds of energy, live just as long, and seem to enjoy life as much if not more. However, their dependence upon three bowls of rice per person per diem undoubtedly accounts for certain special features of the way in which Japanese society developed.

Unlike bulkier, more perishable edibles, rice can be readily transported and stored for considerable periods. Hence it can serve to some degree not only as provender but also as a medium of exchange. Even

before they learned to write their own history, the Japanese knew that
it took about five bushels of rice to fuel one person for one year. This
quantity, called a *koku,* became a measure not only of calories but also
of income and of population. On it, the entire economy including the
system of land ownership and taxation was based from the earliest
times until well into the nineteenth century.

At the start of the Heian period, the imperial government derived
its revenue by exacting in taxes a certain proportion of the rice crop
grown by the entire nation as specified in the Great Reform of A.D.
645. Later, owing to interlocking family relationships, services to the
Crown, or other causes, some owners of large manors or estates began
to be exempted in whole or in part from paying such taxes. Instead,
they were allowed to use these funds for maintaining their own armed
services composed of samurai whose salaries were paid in rice. As
such exemptions became more numerous, the economic strength of the
landed proprietors increased while that of the imperial establishment
dwindled. It was when this process finally tipped the balance in favor
of the landed proprietors that the rise of the Taira and the Minamoto
led to Japan's first great civil war and the consequent elevation of the
shogun to prime political power.

In the civil wars which raged intermittently from the twelfth century
onward, most of the major participants were descendants or collateral
connections of the two original clans. To say that these wars were of
no special consequence to anyone outside Japan is by no means to deny
that for those engaged in fighting them, such contests were not merely
the most important concern but indeed the only important one imagi-
nable. Throughout the Ashikaga era, wars between rival daimyo were
in fact simply a full-time occupation for most of Japan's leading
citizens, just as competition between major companies and corpora-
tions would be for leading citizens of the United States or Europe after
the Industrial Revolution. That, in the former case, the consequences
were more frequently lethal merely meant that, as Karl Marx was
later to note in the case of European feudalism, the stakes included
personal, as well as economic, survival.

When one daimyo, or great-name family, defeated another, the
normal procedure was to take over all or part of its fiefdom, meaning
primarily an appropriate share of the rice produced by its farmers. The

definition of appropriate in this context was a fairly loose one, but in practice it meant all that the farmers did not themselves need in order to survive so as to harvest more rice. The conventional split was *"shi-ko, roku-min,"* or "four to the Prince, six to the people," but the more a great lord could extract from his peasants the more samurai he could employ and the better chance he had of winning his next war. Far from finding this a disagreeable—let alone insupportable—way of life, the daimyo, their samurai retainers, and even the long-suffering farmers who comprised 80 per cent of the population, apparently proceeded on the plausible assumption that there was no other.

From the modern viewpoint, conditioned by the much more destructive wars of the twentieth century, such a state of affairs seems reprehensible if only because, with the peace so incessantly disturbed, not much constructive work could really be accomplished. No such qualms bothered the daimyo or their retainers. For them, fighting each other seemed as natural as breathing, and when the emperor tried to interfere, as he rarely dared, they regarded it more or less in the same way that early twentieth-century capitalists regarded the graduated income tax, as an unwarranted intrusion upon personal liberty.

When Tokugawa Ieyasu finally subdued most of his enemies at the Battle of Sekigahara, the result, to be sure, was a nation more or less at peace, but that had by no means been his primary objective. His aim had been to establish the lasting supremacy of the shogunate; peace was an incidental and perhaps unforeseen by-product. The notion that supremacy could be maintained without fighting, or at least being fully prepared to fight any adversary at any moment, was not one that would have been warmly received by the bakufu. As the third Tokugawa shogun was reported to have said to the leaders of the Shimazu clan on his accession to power in 1623:

"My ancestor and his son regarded you as equals, and you have had certain special privileges. But now I am shogun by right of succession, and you will henceforth be treated as hereditary vassals. If you do not like this . . . then, as tradition dictates, the clash of arms shall decide who is to be supreme in the country."

Just how supreme the Tokugawa actually were can perhaps be most readily perceived by a quick look at the balance sheet. In 1590, when the total rice production in koku, and hence also the national popula-

tion, was reckoned at about 20 million, Ieyasu Tokugawa, as deputy
shogun for Kanto, already held lands whose gross income was assessed
at roughly one million koku. By the time Hideyoshi died in 1598, capital gains resulting from military victories had raised the shogun's
share to two and a half million. The Battle of Sekigahara brought in
almost another four million, making the total about one fourth of the
gross national koku. Ieyasu's heirs continued to build up the family's
holdings so that, by mid-century, the revenue of lands controlled by
direct heirs and related families was about 17 million koku, leaving a
total of some nine million in the hands of the outer daimyo.

By this time, out of a total of some two hundred and sixty fiefs, only
sixty had 100,000 koku or more, and of these only twenty-two belonged
to the "great daimyo" with incomes of over 200,000, among them the
Maeda, the Shimazu, and the Matsudaira. Of the two hundred smaller
fiefs, about half were rated at less than 30,000 koku. While each fief
was comprised of lands in the same general part of the country, most
included numerous separate holdings which might be scattered among
as many as two or three provinces due to intermarriages between separate clans, confiscations after wars, or other contingencies. Excepted
from the tax lists of estates controlled by the daimyo were those whose
income still went to the major Buddhist sects and a few small royal
holdings whose revenues by the start of the eighteenth century had
leveled off at about 40,000 koku.

If the sudden dawn of peace after two hundred years of constant
and multiple civil wars came as a surprise to the daimyo, it was even
more of a shock to the samurai. Originally a class of small independent
landowners who, in return for remittance of their taxes, were prepared
to fight for a local chieftain in time of war, the samurai had long since
become a class of professional warriors who had given up their property rights in exchange for the privilege of wearing two swords and
receiving a salary. The two swords provide a clue to the character of
this class and to the code of ethics called *bushido,* or "way of the warrior"—which was supposed to govern samurai behavior. The long
sword was for cutting off the head of an enemy or cleaving him down
the middle, as the opportunity arose. The short one was to enable its
owner to disembowel himself in the prescribed rite—still sometimes
practiced, as by the writer Yukio Mishima in 1970—called *seppuku,*

Dressed in yukatas, *or informal* kimonos, *six gentle ladies prepare for bed.*

or vulgarly *hara-kiri,* to avoid dishonor or evade defeat in battle.

During the days when the samurai were at their busiest in the epic wars between Taira and Minamoto, the code of bushido remained unwritten because it was still being drafted in action. It began to take documentary shape during the wars of the Muromachi era, and one suspects that, like the Ten Commandments, it may testify more to the prevalence of transgressions against, than to conformity with, the stated code. While opportunities for a minor-league daimyo to change sides arose frequently and on short notice, it was obviously essential from his viewpoint that all his samurai change sides with him—and equally important that they never do so independently. Hence, loyalty, a quality that the daimyo themselves were perhaps inclined to honor more by praise than by precept, was the foundation of the warrior's code—and one with which the conditions of their existence must have made it especially hard to comply.

One difficulty was that, if a chief lost a war, his samurai were out of a job, a circumstance that offered the samurai ample inducement for private preliminary arrangements with the enemy. Another was that, even if a chief prospered in battle, his samurai were still exposed to hardship in years when there might not be enough rice to go around. Between periods of professional activity, employed samurai enjoyed a fairly comfortable existence which included the privilege of slicing up their lower-class compatriots in case they showed traces of insolence. Unemployed samurai, called *ronin,* meaning "men tossed on the waves," had the unappealing options of seppuku, free-lance squabbling, or painful demotion to the ranks of farmers, artisans, or merchants. The large-scale confiscations of the early Tokugawa period naturally created unprecedented swarms of ronin. Their members thus helped expand the merchant class which, as the peace became more contagious and its fruits more plentiful, began to play a bigger role in society. The same cause led to an increase in urban population, of which the most noteworthy beneficiaries were Edo, Kyoto, Osaka, and Nagasaki.

Among the ancillary advantages to the shogun of having channeled all foreign trade through the single port of Nagasaki was that this entitled the bakufu to all revenues produced thereby. Nagasaki became Japan's window on the world and its citizens to some degree more cosmopolitan and sophisticated than their even more isolated compatriots. Kyoto, still the site of the ancient court, kept up pretensions of imperial elegance and refinement. Osaka, whose position on the Inland Sea made it the distribution point for cargoes carried by water to the populous home provinces, became the business and commercial center. Meanwhile, it was Edo as the seat both of shogunal and—since all his vassals were obliged to spend part of their time there—of regional power that became the nation's real capital. Starting as a small village at the beginning of the seventeenth century, it had grown into a metropolis of half a million by the opening of the eighteenth. By the middle of the nineteenth, it was already perhaps, as it certainly is now, the biggest city in the world.

Around the shogun's castle, set in a spacious park about a mile inland from the bay, the town houses of the daimyo were grouped in a wide crescent, most of them on hilltops and each surrounded by a cluster of tradespeople's shops and residential areas for the prosperous merchants and for the warriors who accompanied their lords to and from the capital. In the lower areas between the mansions of the daimyo—around which the districts of modern Tokyo gradually formed—lived poorer citizens whose crowded wooden shanties were periodically consumed by great conflagrations—most notably one in 1657 which was reputed to have cost 100,000 lives. Between the castle and the shore was the mint which—as metal coins gradually replaced rice as a medium of exchange during the seventeenth century—became the locus of a bustling commercial district whose name, *Ginza,* means Silver Place.

With peace suddenly rife in the land, leaving that large segment of the population composed of affluent lords and aristocratic soldiers with little to do, it was inevitable that entertainment, the arts, and pleasure in its more rudimentary forms would find suitable soil in which to flourish. Countryfolk, eager to escape the dreary servitude of rice farming in the provinces, rushed to the cities and especially to Edo to become *chonin,* or townsfolk, from *cho,* meaning a city ward. As artisans, shopkeepers, actors, courtesans, or servants in the great houses, they could participate in the urban pleasures paid for basically by the taxes extracted from the peasants. This transformation reached a peak in the late seventeenth century—in a period known as *Genroku* from the

reign-name of the emperor—but its cultural momentum carried on through the eighteenth century and into the nineteenth.

While the persecution of Japanese Christians under Ieyasu and his successors has naturally attracted more attention from Western historians, a development which may have had more practical importance in Japan was the forcible reduction of the great Buddhist sects by his predecessors Nobunaga and Hideyoshi. Under the Tokugawa, the previously pervasive influence of Buddhism in all its forms was replaced by a renascence in Chinese studies and, through the influence of Confucian philosophy, a return to Shinto. Eager to avoid all taint of Europe and to cling to tradition, the shogunate encouraged developments of this kind; but as peace bred national prosperity, other trends became even more immediately noticeable.

A detail from "The Southern Barbarian Screen" by Kano Naizen shows the arrival of the Portuguese merchants and missionaries.

In literature, the new form that replaced war stories and epics popular with previous generations was the romantic novel, often with a pornographic twist. In poetry, the terse 31-syllable *tanka,* heretofore the most popular form, was further refined by cutting off the last two seven-syllable lines to develop the even more frail and epigrammatic seventeen-syllable *haiku* of which Basho was the most renowned master. In the theater, the Noh drama was replaced by the livelier and more dramatic new form of *kabuki,* derived from what in the old days had been curtain raisers or between-the-acts pantomimes.

Most famous of all the kabuki dramas was the playwright Chikamatsu's classic *Chushingura,* or *Tale of the Forty-Seven Ronin,* a topical treatment of a series of events that started in 1701 when a minor daimyo, provoked into an unseemly quarrel with a retainer of the shogun within the palace walls, was ordered by the bakufu to forfeit his fief and commit seppuku. The daimyo obeyed the verdict, whereupon forty-seven of his now leaderless followers hatched a plot to kill the shogun's retainer which they carried out one snowy February morning in 1702. Ordered to commit seppuku themselves, they promptly did so and were buried together in the yard of a Tokyo temple where their graves still draw thousands of mourners. To Western viewers of the play, a question that often arises is why the forty-seven did not draw lots and let one of their number handle the job, thus sparing the lives of the other forty-six. To ask this question is to miss the point: all of the ronin were equally eager to show their loyalty to their lord.

The *Forty-Seven Ronin,* which still holds a perennial attraction for the Japanese public—like the graves of the ronin themselves—may have owed its original appeal in part to its nostalgic character in a day when the practical relevance of the battlefield virtues it extols was already much less conspicuous. Certainly even for eighteenth-century Edo the focal point of interest was much less any battlefield than the renowned *Yoshiwara,* meaning Happy Fields, a fantastic pleasure quarter whose "splendor was by day like Paradise and by night like the Palace of the Dragon King." Here two thousand or more elegant courtesans and inexpensive trollops competed in ministering to the wants of a male clientele that included rich merchants and seedy samurai, pleasure-loving lords and insomniac artists, writers, and actors, all bent on extra-connubial amusement.

Known also as the *Ukiyo* (Floating World) or *Fuyajo* (Nightless City), the Yoshiwara became the favorite subject of the woodblock print artists of the period whose popular school culminated in the great nineteenth-century masters Hokusai and Hiroshige. Its widely varied play of people and incident also provided the characters and plots for such lively novels as Saikaku's *Man Who Spent His Life Making Love* (1683). And from, though not always of, the pleasure quarter in Edo and other great cities, especially Kyoto, developed that wondrous and enigmatically exquisite creature, the *geisha,* meaning art-person, whose function in Japanese life still seems so mysterious to most Western visitors.

What often puzzles Westerners most about the geisha is that the arts she seems most eager to demonstrate at a gathering arranged by their Japanese hosts are handkerchief tricks or children's parlor games like "scissor cuts paper, paper wraps stone" which he may find less than breathtakingly exciting as a form of sexual enticement. Here again this is to miss the point. On the plane of physical sexuality, Japanese wives appear from the available evidence to be just as satisfactory to their mates as their Western counterparts, if not more so. Their fault is that they are less satisfactory on some other planes. Hence, what a well-to-do Japanese husband usually wants to find in a night on the town is not an instant bedmate so much as a feminine companion capable of carrying on an amusing conversation as well as being attractive to look at and, perhaps eventually, make love to. One reason that contemporary geisha find themselves obliged to resort to infantile games with Westerners is, of course, simply that the latter are as a rule hopelessly incapable of understanding any Japanese conversation whatsoever.

As for the geisha's elaborately traditional dress and hairdo, which are also more likely to puzzle than please most foreigners, it may be helpful to consider the peculiar susceptibility of Japanese men to such esoteric points of feminine attraction as, in dress, the wide sash called an *obi* and, in anatomy, the nape of the neck. Both of these unlikely idiosyncrasies may seem somewhat less puzzling when it is recalled, in the light of Freud's well-known pleasure principle, that most Japanese men during infancy enjoyed being carried around on their mothers' backs attached thereto by a wide sash in such a way that the back of the maternal neck necessarily becomes a subject of close and prolonged scrutiny. In any event, the fact that conjugal social life remained unknown in Japan during the entire shogunal period may make both the character and the vast popularity of the Yoshiwara considerably more intelligible. That social events at which both sexes are represented remain a rarity in Japan also helps account for the character of the innumerable little bars and tearooms along the Ginza which, perhaps rather regrettably, have come to be the Yoshiwara's closest present-day equivalent.

That life in the great cities of Japan must have been exciting and enjoyable may be deduced not only from indigenous sources but also from the excellent description provided by a rarely privileged European visitor named Engelbert Kaempfer. As a German physician attached to the Dutch trading community in Deshima, he accompanied his hosts in 1691 and 1692 on the duty call to Edo which they, like the daimyo, were expected to pay every year. Kaempfer kept a journal of both his visits and in them provides an enlightening report on much that he saw including a minor earthquake, the execution grounds near Edo where samurai were allowed to practice their sword play on the rotting corpses, and a typical Edo fire that consumed six hundred houses. One detail that especially caught Kaempfer's eye was the dense traffic encountered along the Tokaido, the famous highway from Tokyo to Osaka, which confirms the impression later to be conveyed by Hiroshige in his famous series of woodblock prints showing daimyo, samurai, merchants, peasants, innkeepers, tavern girls, porters, and all other ingredients of the lively scene at the way stations along the road.

The high point of the 1692 visit came when the members of the Dutch mission were received at the palace of the then shogun Tsunayoshi, where the ladies of the court were permitted to peek at them through a slitted screen. Kaempfer reported what followed:

"He ordered us to take off . . . our Garment of Ceremony, then to stand upright, that he might have a full view of us; again to walk, to stand still, to compliment each other, to dance, to jump, to play the drunkard, to speak broken Japanese, to read Dutch, to paint, to sing, to put our cloaks on and off. Meanwhile we obeyed the Emperor's commands in the best manner we could. I joined to my dance a love song in High German. In this manner and with innumerable other such apish tricks, we must suffer ourselves to contribute to the . . . court's diversion."

Another detail—about which Kaempfer may have been mistaken—was the well-being of the peasants and farmers he saw along the way, perhaps because he did not have much time to talk to them. While he seems to have found them in the best of health and spirits, both contemporary records and modern research convey a somewhat less cheerful picture. Most of them were taxed to the utmost limit of endurance, so that both the sale of children into slavery and *mabiki*—"thinning out," a euphemism for infanticide—were so widely practiced that laws had to be passed in an effort to control them. In addition, countryfolk experienced severe periodic famines due partly to real scarcity of rice and partly to inadequate transport. In years of poor crops, mass starvation sometimes wiped out whole villages.

The underlying purposes of the early Tokugawa shoguns in ejecting the Europeans, disciplining the daimyo, and stabilizing the existing order of things in the early seventeenth century was, of course, in essence a conservative one. The reason that Ieyasu and his successors wished to prevent outsiders from coming in was primarily because they hoped to maintain the status quo. If history had only one lesson to teach, it would be that this objective is unattainable. In this case, the change thus brought about proved to be proportionate to the efficiency of the efforts to prevent any change whatsoever. By stabilizing a country that had never known stability, what the Tokugawa finally achieved was a revolution more complete than any that had preceded it.

In 1600 Japan had been less a nation than a loose conglomeration of tiny principalities comprising some 20 million inhabitants whose main occupation, next to raising rice, was making war on each other. By the middle of the nineteenth century, it was a peaceful and unified mercantile nation whose population had leveled off at 30 million due to mortality from sources far removed from warfare. About the only thing that had not altered was the government—but by 1853, the time was entirely ripe for that.

I n an era when electronic communication makes instantaneously visible on one side of the globe events that are occurring on the other, it becomes increasingly hard to imagine a world in which it was possi-

Japanese theater and dance are known for their colorful spectacle: at right, the masklike face of a kagura dancer; below, members of the wealthy merchant class at a performance of the beloved kabuki theater.

ble, not only for Europe to thrive without being aware that there were such places as Mexico and Peru, but also for Peru and Mexico to be wholly ignorant of each others' existence until the Spaniards arrived to convey the news. Thus, while Europe was uninformed about, and hence unaffected by, all the furious commotion that was going on in Japan from the arrival of Jimmu Tenno to that of Saint Francis Xavier, the serenity of the Tokugawa centuries in Japan was in no way diminished by developments that shook the rest of the world. The American Revolution and the Napoleonic Wars had as little discernible impact there as the epic struggle between the Taira and the Minamoto had had upon Europe during the reign of England's Henry II. Nonetheless, no island is really an island unto itself; and the bell that would signal an end to this happy state of affairs began to toll from outside not long after the period of unwonted serenity began.

With the British, Spanish, and Portuguese effectively ruled out of the picture, the next major efforts to get in touch with the Japanese came from a source much nearer to hand—Russia. While other nations of Europe had been expanding eastward by sea, Russia had been doing likewise more slowly and by land, across the barren wastes of Siberia. A half century or so after Japan had slammed the front door shut at Nagasaki, Russians found themselves in a position to knock on the back one, at the northern island of Hokkaido, then known as Ezo.

Moscow had first heard about Ezo from a Japanese sailor named Dembei who, shipwrecked on the Kamchatka coast, was taken to the capital in 1702 to be received by Peter the Great. Several attempts to develop relations with Japan via the Kamchatka Peninsula and the Kurile Islands took place during the decades that followed but none of them had much effect until 1792. Then, during the reign of Catherine the Great, a young Russian lieutenant named Adam Laxman put in at the Ezo port of Nemuro and sent a letter to Edo indicating that he was authorized to open negotiations for trade.

Laxman's application eventually brought a reply advising him that foreigners could only be received through Nagasaki and that he should present himself there. A few years later, a more senior representative in the person of Admiral Nikolai Rezanov did apply at Nagasaki, only to be informed after a wait of several months that his admission was denied. Partly because of pique on Rezanov's part and partly in the hope of forcing a more conciliatory tone, Russian ships thereafter made raids on the port towns of Ezo and Sakhalin. These achieved nothing except possibly to help account for the reception accorded the next official visit by Russians. This was a call by a cruiser which in 1811 came all the way from the Baltic Sea under command of a captain named Vasili Golovnin—Rezanov having by this time set off to found colonies in Alaska and California. When Golovnin and several of his officers went ashore on Ezo, they were promptly carried off to prison and kept there for two years before being allowed to rejoin their ship and sail home.

During the time that Captain Golovnin and his comrades spent on Ezo, the British warship H.M.S. *Phaeton* sailed into Nagasaki hoping to happen on a merchant ship from the Netherlands, then under Napoleonic rule. Irked to find no enemy merchantman in port, the *Phaeton*'s dashing young skipper, Lieutenant Fleetwood Pellew, demanded food supplies and threatened to sink every vessel in the harbor if they were not promptly provided. The governor of Nagasaki furnished the supplies and then, the evening after the *Phaeton* had departed, committed seppuku out of shame for his inability to resist. Subsequent calls by importunate British ships at other coastal cities on both the main islands and the Ryukyus led to comparably regrettable incidents. The bakufu responded by ordering local authorities to fire upon any ship that came close to shore and to arrest or kill any crew members who might try to land.

Last of all the great nations to begin casting over the Japanese pool was the United States, whose first serious effort took place in 1837. Some Japanese fishermen who had been blown off course and cast ashore on the west coast of Canada had been dispatched, via Britain, to Macao where they attracted the attention of United States businessmen and missionaries based at Canton. The latter groups chartered a small vessel named the *Morrison* to try to repatriate the fishermen and, if a chance arose, also to drum up a little trade. When the unarmed *Morrison* attempted to discharge her errand of mercy tempered by profit, she was fired upon first at the entrance to Edo Bay, and then at Kagoshima, obliging her to return with the unhappy passengers still on board. An American supercargo later on published a book about the incident which served its purpose of arousing congressmen, church

dignitaries, and other domestic opinion makers to the necessity for "opening up" Japan.

When news of what the *Morrison* had been trying to do reached the bakufu, its previous orders were revoked. Port authorities were instructed not to fire upon foreign ships but rather to give them the supplies they asked for and then merely advise them to depart. Shortly thereafter, however, news arrived through Nagasaki of Britain's Opium War with China and subsequent acquisition of Hong Kong. This swung the pendulum back the other way, causing the nervous bakufu to make efforts to strengthen coastal defenses. Using books acquired from Dutch sources at Nagasaki, they drilled two companies of troops in what was deduced to be the approved Western style.

During the first half of the eighteenth century, oil for the lamps of American kitchens, not to mention machinery in general, came from the sperm whales which United States whalers hunted in the North Pacific. Ships engaged in this hazardous enterprise were not infrequently blown ashore on the Japanese islands or obliged to put in at Japanese ports to ask for shelter or supplies. Reports by sailors lucky enough to survive the rough treatment they received there—and also,

At left, a woodblock print from 1853 shows four foreign steamships entering Nagasaki harbor. At right, Admiral Perry is greeted by the governor of Uraga.

perhaps, their accounts of the Japanese prosperity of which they had meanwhile caught a glimpse—stirred further interest in the matter. In 1846 Commodore James Biddle, returning from a voyage to Canton, was instructed to put in at Edo and deliver a letter from the president.

This visit proved to be a fiasco. As a Philadelphia patrician accustomed to trying hard not to be stuffy with strangers, Biddle leaned too far in the opposite direction, handing his letter to a minor official, letting sightseers clamber all over his ships, and finally obeying instructions to come aboard a Japanese guard boat to receive the shogun's reply. The reply, which was rudely transmitted and came from the governor of Uraga rather than the shogun, ordered him to leave and never come back. Having been instructed to do nothing that might "excite a hostile feeling," Biddle meekly complied. In the absence of a breeze, it then became necessary to have his becalmed ships ignominiously towed out of the harbor by Japanese guard boats.

At about the time of Biddle's visit, there occurred another incident of a totally different nature which also had some bearing on developments. This was the rescue by a United States whaling ship of a fourteen-year-old Japanese castaway named Manjiro. The whaler took him back to New Bedford, Massachusetts, and for two years Manjiro went to school in nearby Fairhaven. He then joined the Gold Rush to California, failed to make a strike, and took ship for Honolulu where he encountered two other rescued compatriot castaways. The three together made an attempt to get home via the Ryukyus where Manjiro was arrested and sent to Kagoshima for questioning by the daimyo. Interested in his account of his travels, the daimyo dispatched him to the shogun who, instead of having his head chopped off, raised him to samurai rank and made him a court translator.

Among the items of information which Manjiro was able to convey to the shogun, one was that the United States had no imperialistic designs upon Japan. Another was that, as a result of a war with Mexico, the United States had recently acquired California—and with it a vastly increased concern with the Pacific. By mid-century this concern had in fact been further intensified by the advent of steam propulsion, which suggested that a coaling station in the North Pacific would be a handy if not essential aid to the rapidly increasing trade with China. In 1853 Commodore Matthew Calbraith Perry, a gruff but diplomatically seasoned officer known to his crews as "Old Bruin," received from President Millard Fillmore the order that was perhaps that dignitary's major contribution to world history. This was to take a squadron of warships around the Cape of Good Hope, across the Indian Ocean, and into Edo Harbor, there to deliver a letter to the Japanese emperor that would set matters straight.

Where Perry's visit to Japan differed from that of Biddle and all his predecessors since 1640 was that he not only knew what he wanted but exactly how to go about getting it. On July 8, 1853, his four ships, bristling with bigger guns than any Japanese had seen before, swung along the coast of the Izu Peninsula and into the entrance of Edo Bay. The ships were in line-ahead formation—two steam frigates towing two others with sails furled—so that their guns covered all shore batteries. Just before their anchors rattled down, their sailors saw the snowcapped cone of Mount Fuji appear through the summer mists, glittering high above the wooded hills along the shore line.

To thousands of onlookers along the coast, the most amazing thing about these Black Ships, whose hulls were in fact painted black above the water line, was that they had come into the harbor against the wind. The smoke pouring from the funnels of the two steam frigates caused rumors to circulate that they were on fire and needed help. When they stopped moving, and this proved unfounded, Japanese guard boats surrounded them, their crews clamoring to come aboard. Perry had given orders that no one was to board any ship except his flagship, the *Susquehanna,* and then only some responsible officer. When a Japanese functionary accompanied by a Dutch interpreter came alongside the *Susquehanna* asking to see Perry, the reply was that the commodore "would see no one but a Mandarin of the highest rank, and that he might return on shore."

"I was well aware," Perry later reported to Washington, "that the more exclusive I should make myself and the more exacting I might be, the more respect these people of forms and ceremonies would be disposed to award me. . . ."

That night, according to the officer on watch from midnight to 4 A.M., an amazing meteor was seen which "made its appearance in the south and west and illuminated the whole atmosphere. . . . Its shape was that of a large blue sphere with a red wedge-shaped tail. . . . The ancients would have construed this . . . as an omen promising a favorable issue to an enterprise undertaken by them, and we may pray God that our present attempt to bring a singular and half barbarous people into the family of civilized nations, may succeed without resort to bloodshed."

It did so succeed, though by no means all at once. After a week of parleys with representatives of the bakufu whom Perry deemed of appropriate rank, he was enabled to deliver his letter from the president, with due ceremony and with the understanding that he would return in the spring for a reply. Asked whether he would bring all four ships back with him, Old Bruin growled a characteristic response: "Probably more."

True to his word, he returned the next spring with a flotilla of nine. This time, the bakufu was prepared to accede to the demands of the president's letter by opening the ports of Shimoda and Hakkodate to limited trade with United States ships and providing for a United States Consulate. Within two years, the treaty had been followed by similar agreements with Britain, Russia, and Holland; and Japan's two hundred and fifty years of exclusion had come to an abrupt end.

CHAPTER V

GUNS OF THE
ISLAND DWARFS

I nasmuch as the United States had instigated the "opening up" of
Japan, with much resounding talk about the urgent need for international trade, coaling stations in the North Pacific, and suitable amenities for shipwrecked whalers, one might have supposed that Perry's
feats would have received front-page coverage in the American press
and that his return to New York, where he had a handsome new house
on Thirty-Ninth Street, might have been the occasion for the contemporary equivalent of a ticker tape welcome. Nothing of the sort took
place. When Perry got back to the United States via Europe, after
handing over his ships to a successor in Hong Kong, the event passed
almost unnoticed. His own report of his accomplishment, published in
book form just before his death in 1858, achieved a modest sale, but
it was not until well after the Civil War that Japan's new status aroused
much interest in the country chiefly responsible for it. In Japan, on the
other hand, according to an authoritative eyewitness report by the
historian Katsu Awa, "From the day of Perry's arrival for more than
ten years our country was in a state of indescribable confusion." This
was perhaps something of an understatement.

*The once-proud samurai had lost both privilege and purpose when this nine-
teenth-century photograph was taken.*

The confusion caused by Perry's arrival was by no means the result of mere surprise. In fact the bakufu had received ample warning of his coming from two widely diverse sources. One was the Dutch trading post at Deshima to which information about Perry's expedition had been relayed by the Netherlands Embassy in Washington a year ahead of time. The other was Okinawa in the Ryukyu Islands where Perry had stopped off for two weeks en route and whose regent had sent a detailed report to his lord, the daimyo of Satsuma. The cause of the confusion was rather that, given the news of the impending arrival, no one in Edo had the slightest idea what to do about it, with the possible exception of the shogun himself.

In the long line of Tokugawa scions since Ieyasu there had been several inept and ailing occupants of the shogunal throne. The twelfth, who was ruling in 1853, while perhaps abler than the ninth, or "bed-wetting shogun," who had ruled from 1745 to 1760, was nonetheless one of this number; when the Black Ships arrived no one could even think how to break the news to him. When he learned of Perry's arrival by accident three days later during a private performance of Noh drama at the palace, the shock sent him to his bed where he expired a few days after Perry's departure, leaving matters in the hands of the *roju,* or council of elders.

Aboard the heavily armed ships which accompanied Perry on his return in 1854 were some sixteen hundred sailors, amounting to about one quarter of the entire personnel of the United States Navy at the time. Twenty thousand Japanese soldiers had been hastily called to arms, but their fire power was limited to thirty old-fashioned muskets per thousand. The Japanese were moreover under the erroneous impression that Perry also had at his disposal fifty additional warships in nearby waters and fifty more available on short notice from California. And on top of all this, between Perry's first visit and his second, four Russian warships commanded by Admiral Putiatin had turned up in Nagasaki to make demands, similar to Perry's, for one or more open ports and a trade treaty. The Russians had been sent off with a firm refusal; nonetheless, it had become apparent that foreign pressure was being applied from all sides and that something would have to be done forthwith. The vexing question that remained was: what?

A poll of fifty-nine leading daimyo just after Perry's departure in

1853 had shown that about one third favored accepting the proposal for trade with the United States, another third favored rejecting it, and the remainder favored an unlikely compromise of postponing a decision and strengthening the nation's defenses. With this helpful consensus on hand, the bakufu understandably felt inclined to request advice from every other conceivable source including that of the madam of the best-known bordello in the Yoshiwara. Her ingenious suggestion was to send soldiers out to the ships disguised as peddlers. They would then go aboard, get the crews drunk, blow up the powder magazines, and in the consequent uproar, dispose of the sailors with short knives. (Although not accepted, her proposal was not much more extravagant than one that had been acted upon on the occasion of Perry's earlier visit: a squad of nine samurai had hidden themselves under the platform of the reception house where Perry met Japanese officials to deliver his letter from President Fillmore. If any of the visitors had shown signs of aggressive action, these concealed warriors were to have dashed out and cut them to pieces with their long swords.)

The intense and localized confusion inside the bakufu at the time of Perry's second visit and in the ensuing months was symptomatic of a much deeper and wider disruption in the country as a whole that was to manifest itself increasingly throughout the decade that followed. This disruption was the consequence of the bakufu's failure to react to social changes during the 250-year Tokugawa regime. By 1853 most peasants who had not moved into the towns were bitterly discontented with their lot; the samurai were, in effect, an entire class of unemployed patricians; and the daimyo were hopelessly in debt to the rich merchants, whose daughters their sons frequently married in an effort to improve their financial position. The merchants, accordingly, now exerted an influence totally inconsistent with their nominal rank below samurai, artisans, and peasants. The crisis caused by Perry's arrival—and the bakufu's unprecedented display of indecision in inviting the opinions of the daimyo—was the signal for the start of a long-delayed social upheaval. The prime movers, as might have been expected, were the outer daimyo of the southwest provinces led by the traditionally dissident lords of Choshu and Satsuma.

The widespread confusion was compounded by the death of the twelfth shogun which created a new series of problems concerning the ultimate succession. The thirteenth shogun was Iesada, whose age and character made it unlikely that he would produce an heir. The two leading candidates for this position were therefore Tokugawa Iemochi, who was Iesada's first cousin, and Tokugawa Keiki, whose father was the powerful lord of Mito. The consequent rivalry for the shogunal throne was eventually settled in favor of Iemochi, but not before it had caused another division among the daimyo, intersecting the one already created by the question of what to do about the foreigners. As a means of resolving both at once, the outer daimyo had recourse to a notion unheard of since Go-Daigo had made his ill-fated attempt to reassert imperial power. In the years that immediately followed Perry's visits, the leaders of this group, who were geographically closer to Kyoto than to the scene of the Black Ships' intrusion, became allied under the slogan *"Sonno Joi"* ("Revere the Emperor, expel the Barbarians"). The result was increasingly bitter conflict between them and the group of Tokugawa daimyo who, being closer to Edo, had seen more reason to endorse the bakufu's acceptance of Perry's proposal.

The bitterness of the conflict became evident first in a series of atrocities committed by antiforeign samurai at the expense of the newly arrived European community. These included the murder of a Chinese servant in the French consulate, of an English-speaking Japanese interpreter in the British legation, and then of the amiable Henricus Heusken, secretary to the United States consul Townsend Harris who, in 1856, had become the first foreigner to take up actual residence in Japan. It reached a climax in March, 1860, with the assassination of Ii Naosuke, the bakufu's *tairo,* or prime minister, who had signed the 1858 treaty drafted by Harris to itemize and amplify the privileges of trade and residence called for in the earlier agreement drafted by Perry. When the shogunate proved too timorous to arrest and punish the perpetrators of the latter crime, the movement to eliminate the shogun himself gained momentum, with the daimyo of Satsuma and Choshu now joined by those of Tosa and Hizen. All four names were combined to give the alliance its designation of Satcho-Dohi.

During the early and middle sixties, the indescribable confusion referred to by Katsu Awa came to include not only intermittent multiple civil wars between factions of factions, reminiscent of the Muromachi days preceding the Tokugawa, but also international incidents comparable to those which elsewhere in Asia had led to alien occupations. The most dramatic developments among the latter were the bombardment of the Satsuma capital of Kagoshima by British warships, in retaliation for the slicing up of a British trader named Richardson near Yokohama by a Shimazu swordsman in 1863; and, a year later, the bombardment of the Choshu clan's forts commanding Shimonoseki Strait by a combined fleet of foreign vessels in retaliation for attacks on all foreign ships that had dared use the waterway.

During the earlier years of the nineteenth century, the once seemingly boundless wealth of the Tokugawa had suffered a sudden and alarming decline. Caused first by extravagance on the part of incompetent rulers, later by declining revenues from financially embarrassed daimyo, and most recently by the new expenses of trying to contain peasant revolts and to bolster national defenses, this had led to deficits which the bakufu had hoped to recoup through tariffs on foreign trade. While the combined total of imports and exports had grown from less than $2,000,000 in 1859 to over $30,000,000 in 1865, efforts to tax either one had proved ineffective, and the bakufu was still running an annual deficit of 700,000 gold *ryo,* or the rough equivalent of that many koku of rice per year. When the clansmen of Choshu, whose west coast fiefdom comprised the two important provinces of Nagato and Suo and whose provincial armies were equipped with the newest type of imported firearms, broke into open revolt in 1866, the shogunate was driven to seek financial aid abroad. After trying in vain to float a $6,000,000 loan in Paris, it suffered a serious defeat in the field. By the spring of 1866 the stage was set for a major civil war between the Satcho-Dohi and the tottering bakufu.

The equivalent of a "divine wind" which rescued Japan from its dire predicament this time was the conveniently coincident demise, first in August, 1866, of the shogun Iemochi, and then in the following January, of the emperor Komei. The new shogun was Iemochi's former rival for the succession, Keiki, who proved to be an amiable, not to say irresolute, young man whose interests did not include putting up a serious fight to preserve the power of his ancestral office. With the Tokugawa's traditional and long-dreaded internal enemies firmly allied against him in an overpowering coalition poised to attack his Edo castle, Keiki gratefully accepted the peace conditions offered by the emperor's ablest general, a renowned Satsuma warrior named Saigo Takamori. These included his abdication, which put an end not merely to the two-and-a-half century reign of the Tokugawa shogunate but to the entire bakufu system which had ruled Japan for almost a full millennium.

While the real name of the emperor who, at the age of fifteen, succeeded Komei was Mutsuhito, his reign name was Meiji, meaning "Enlightened Rule." It is as the Meiji emperor or, to the European world, as Emperor Meiji, that he was to become during the next forty-five years by far the most widely renowned representative of his ancient line. Even before he acquired the throne, Meiji had been surrounded by a coterie of the ablest samurai of the Satcho-Dohi group, most of whom, though more than twice the age of their ruler, were still young men themselves. These counselors—among whom the most renowned were Iwakura, Okubo, Kido, Okuma, Yamagata, and Ito—came to constitute, with the emperor himself as he grew older, the effective government of Japan for the next four decades. By the time they acquired executive power they had recognized that if there had ever been a chance of expelling the barbarian, it had long since vanished. Instead of making further efforts in that direction, they accepted the situation and transferred the royal capital from Kyoto, where it had remained since Heian days, to the shogun's former palace at Edo.

To complete the confusion, at least insofar as foreigners were concerned, the new capital was given the name of the old one in approximate phonetic reverse—Tōkyō, as opposed to Kyōto—in characters showing that while the latter meant "Capital City" the former meant "Eastern Capital." In Tokyo the new monarch made it clear that henceforth the national policy would be not merely to tolerate the presence of foreigners but to learn from them with the same hungry enthusiasm that Yamato Japan had shown in learning from the Chinese a millennium before—and with even more noteworthy success.

While the outcome of Perry's negotiations with the Japanese was no doubt in part attributable to his authoritative demeanor and to the warships with which he could have reinforced it if the need had arisen, he had also taken pains on his second visit to bring along a carrot as well as a stick. The carrot took the form of a rich bag of presents including a barrel of whiskey for the shogun, mirrors and French perfumes for his wife, and, for his subordinates, a crateful of Colt revolvers, lifeboats, potatoes, and best of all a telegraph set and a model train. The former could send real messages and the latter, being a quarter of life-size, was big enough for a person to ride on.

As set forth by Samuel Eliot Morison in his admirable biography of the commodore, Perry had chosen these gifts with characteristic care. The model train included a 350-foot, 18-inch gauge track on which it could run around in a circle at 20 miles per hour. The telegraph set, about which he had corresponded at length with its inventor, Samuel F. B. Morse, was installed to operate between Yokohama and a nearby village. During the treaty negotiations, Japanese dignitaries spent much of their time whizzing around in circles on the tiny locomotive, their robes flying as they clung to the cab. Visitors of all sorts stood in line to send messages to friends by means of the telegraph line. The effect of these toys went far beyond their immediate success. Through word-of-mouth description and woodblock prints that received nationwide distribution, they gave a festive note to the whole visit. To many Japanese it began to seem possible that the outside world, instead of being a threatening wilderness, might be an enchanting wonderland, worth not only trading with but exploring in person.

For a nation which, more than a thousand years before, had gone

A netsuke *depicting Daruma, the legendary Buddhist saint who lost the use of his legs after long meditation.*

so eagerly to school in China, this feeling helped make the years after Perry in one sense a renascence or a re-creation of the Heian mood on a vastly enlarged and accelerated scale. Might not Europe and the United States be a kind of exaggerated latter-day China from which it would now be possible to acquire not merely a language but magical new capabilities of all sorts of which the marvellous wireless and loco-motive were typical examples? Beneath all the indescribable confusion that followed Perry's visits, there was the characteristic Japanese exuberance which carried into every kind of activity and gave the new age its essential character. For some clue as to how the Japanese of the first millennium bridged the gap between the Stone Age and *Genji Monogatari* in one huge jump—or how their contemporary compatri-ots have contrived to convert defeat in World War II to their present fantastic commercial success—the student of Japanese history need only observe what happened in the nation between 1860 and the start of the twentieth century.

Even before the Meiji restoration, during the bakufu's last uneasy years, this eager, not to say voracious, spirit of acceptance had found expression in a series of missions comparable to those of the eighth and ninth centuries to the T'ang capital at Ch'ang-an except that these later missions made multiple calls at Washington, London, Paris, Rome, Berlin, and Petrograd. The first one took off in 1860 for an eastward round-the-world trip, of which the ostensible purpose was to ratify the treaty signed by Townsend Harris in 1858. The actual objective was to look over the whole situation and bring back a full report. The diary of this mission, kept by a delegate named Muragaki Awaji-no-Kami, may be almost as enlightening for modern readers as it was for his own contemporaries in Japan upon its first publication.

Muragaki's report opens with the arrival of the mission in San Fran-cisco aboard the *Powhatan,* which had been Perry's flagship in 1854. There, its ninety-three members put up at the Matheson International Hotel where they gaped with astonishment at such amenities as beds, newspapers, and chamberpots, which one member of the group—understandably in view of their resemblance to porcelain Japanese headrests—mistook for pillows. From San Francisco, port of entry for the energetic Chinese immigrants who were then still engaged in com-pleting the rail link with the East Coast, the group proceeded to

Emperor Meiji, who gave his name to a period of political and social reform

Panama where they saw a full-size railroad train for the first time. The ensuing ride across the isthmus made a deep impression:

"The train was released and started. As it sped like an arrow we could not distinguish the trees and plants on either side of the road. The noise sounded like a thousand peals of thunder over one's head and no matter with how loud a voice one spoke he still could not be understood. But the cars did not rock and they went very fast. . . . The distance of 57 miles . . . was covered in three hours. The reader will please consider this great speed. . . ."

In Washington the group was received by President James Buchanan and attended a ball given by Secretary of State Lewis Cass:

"Officers in uniform with epaulets and swords and ladies dressed in gowns of light white material began, couple by couple, moving around the room, walking on tiptoe to the tune of music. They went round and round as nimbly as so many white mice on their monotonous walk, without making fluttering gestures with their hands even. . . . We were told that this was what is called a 'waltz'. . . ."

Even more revealing in some respects than the report of the mission secretary was that of a much more sophisticated young man named Fukuzawa Yukichi who went along as aide to one of the senior dignitaries. Like a good many other residents of the southwestern provinces during the last years of Tokugawa rule, Fukuzawa had learned Dutch, attended a Nagasaki school in which European science was taught, and picked up considerable knowledge of Western ways—certainly much more than his hosts in Europe and the United States were inclined to credit him with. His impressions of San Francisco, then not much more than an oversize mining camp, were often at variance with those of the older members of the group:

"There was as yet no railway laid to the city. . . . But the telegraph system and also Galvani's electroplating were already in use. . . . We were taken to a sugar refinery and had the principle of the operation explained to us quite minutely. I am sure that our hosts thought they were showing us something entirely new, naturally looking for our surprise at each new device of modern engineering. But, on the contrary, there was nothing really new, at least to me. . . . I had been studying nothing else but such scientific principles ever since I had entered Ogata's school. . . ."

Some clue to the Japanese reading public's interest in the Western world was its response to the book which Fukuzawa wrote about his trip, in which he discussed the political systems of various European nations, compared their religions, philosophies, and social customs, and pointed out that Japan might have a lot to learn from England in particular, as an island country in a somewhat similar setting. A first printing of 150,000 copies sold out rapidly and subsequent editions continued to appear until the turn of the century.

The success of the first mission and the public interest in its findings would doubtless have been enough to ensure many more such expeditions, even without the prompting of the Heian example. As in the earlier situation, one purpose of the travelers was to search out the most important subjects to which Japanese students should address themselves and the sources to which they should apply. Another was to make arrangements for bringing European and American experts to Japan, to provide on-the-spot instruction and do-it-yourself courses for local officials, governmental or private as the case might be.

When the British insisted that the Japanese install lightships and harbor beacons to help foreign vessels find their way past danger spots along the coast and into the narrow craggy harbors, the Japanese not only agreed with alacrity but imported a British specialist named Henry Brunton to help them attend to this task. Brunton arrived in 1868 with two assistants, stayed for eight years, and wrote a book about his experiences which presently came to include a wide variety of innovations other than maritime illumination. From his impatient description of his hosts' overeagerness, it is easy to infer the mood with which Japan was adapting to Western ways:

"High officers of the government, feudal barons and all who could command sufficient means purchased steamboats. . . . Unfortunately for these first purchasers, steamboats are extremely intricate and, in the hands of the ignorant, dangerous instruments both as regards their guidance across the sea and their internally propelling machinery. Heedless of the fact that their own people were without experience in controlling or working them, the Japanese owners placed unskilled persons in charge of the vessels, usually with frequent results of a disastrous character."

Further data on the rapidity with which events moved during the

first years of the Meiji restoration can be gleaned from the back files of the newspaper *Mainichi,* which first appeared in 1866 and was itself a Western innovation patterned both on European models and on the English-language *Nagasaki Shipping List and Advertiser* which had started in 1860. November of 1868 marked the publication of the first serviceable English-Japanese dictionary. In 1869 Japan sent displays to the London World's Fair, and a naval academy, staffed largely by British officers, was founded by imperial edict. The year 1871 was a banner year for social progress in which postal service was started and Far Eastern Feminine Liberation took its first uncertain steps with the departure of five upper-class girls to study in U.S. schools and colleges while their less affluent sisters were cheered by the news that pleasure houses in the Yoshiwara would soon be built in Western style.

In 1872 the number of *rickshaws*—two-wheeled, man-powered passenger carts—had reached a total of 40,000 in Tokyo alone. When

These sober gentlemen comprised the first Japanese diplomatic mission to the United States, in 1860.

the governor of the northern province of Akita was bold enough to go for a drive in his new carriage, crowds formed in the streets and cried out in alarm: "A rickshaw drawn by a horse!" In that year also Japan adopted the standard Georgian calendar; and the first full-size ocean-going ship built there in over two centuries reached San Francisco on its maiden voyage. By 1873, though foreign street dress was still such a novelty that it caused dogs to bark, the once-forbidden eating of meat had become so widespread in Tokyo that a score of cows were slaughtered daily. In that year too, the first national bank was launched with a capital of 3,000,000 yen. By 1876 a government office had bought an ice-cream freezer and mail was being exchanged with the U.S.

In 1872, less than twenty years after Perry had exhibited his toy wireless and model train on the beach at Yokohama, the foreign colony there numbered approximately a thousand, and a genuine railroad with eighteen miles of track and ten locomotives linked the port with the capital. Its gala opening had been attended by the emperor himself, and several trains a day made the run in less than an hour. By the end of the decade, trackage had reached 128 miles and linked several of the main towns along the Pacific coast. During the seventies, telegraph wires were being strung all over the country despite the belief of some cynical peasants that their purpose was to transmit blood to quench the thirst of the red-haired barbarians. After the farmers had overcome their early suspicions of the device, a further problem arose when some hung baskets of rice on the wire in hope that, since it could carry messages, it could also carry their produce to market for them.

Despite such minor misunderstandings, the Japanese had certain enormous advantages over Europe in coping with the Industrial Revolution. Chief among these was a disciplined population whose major element—the 80 per cent composed of farmers—was prepared not only to accept industrialization but to snatch at this chance to escape from precarious drudgery in the rice fields to the relative ease and comfort of jobs in primitive factories. However, while artisans and merchants also welcomed the change, and while the limited ranks of the daimyo were equipped to adjust as need be, there was still one class that found the switch from Tokugawa feudalism to nineteenth-century industrialization highly distasteful. This was the fierce, proud, two-sworded samurai who, though eventually destined for a satisfactory role in the new Japan as what sociologists might call its upper-middle to middle-upper class, were by no means prepared to give up their previously more exalted status without a sharp and characteristically bloody struggle.

The troubles of the samurai, which started soon after the restoration, had economic roots. The dilemma that confronted the Meiji regime as soon as it took office was that of finding an acceptable alternative to the antiquated arrangements whereby the daimyo collected taxes in rice and then expended the grain on dues to the bakufu and stipends to their samurai. In 1873 this was solved when the daimyo, led by the enlightened lords of Satsuma and Choshu, voluntarily handed over their fiefdoms to the Crown, receiving in exchange lump sum capital grants based on the value of their holdings. Along with the grants, they were awarded titles based on European models whereby the heads of the richest families like the Shimazu or the Maeda, with incomes of one million koku or more, became princes while their more modestly affluent colleagues became barons, counts, or viscounts. Meanwhile, a nationwide land survey and appraisal, unprecedented since the one conducted by Emperor Kotoku in 645, gave the Crown a dependable revenue from direct land taxes and thus the means to establish a system of government finance based on an annual budget.

Unhappily slighted in the new economic order were the million or so samurai who, completely deprived of their traditional stipend, were first offered in exchange government bonds bearing interest amounting to about half their previous income. Later, these pensions were recalled and replaced by an even less generous lump-sum settlement intended to enable the samurai to get a new start in life. At the same time these proud warriors were deprived of their right not only to use their hereditary swords for carving up any peasant who failed to show respect, but also, except for special occasions, even to wear them.

Some of the samurai had by this time already descended, however reluctantly, to taking jobs in industry or commerce. Others, especially those in the clans most closely associated with the restoration, found posts in government or as officers in either the new conscript army, the burgeoning navy, or the nationalized police force. Many thousands, however, remained as an unruly ronin element of unprecedented proportions. Of these dispossessed retainers, a substantial number congregated in Satsuma, where the renowned Saigo Takamori, himself far from satisfied with the way things were being run in Tokyo, had set up a sort of private West Point or Sandhurst designed to turn the samurai into a national officer class.

Since Saigo enjoyed the status of a national as well as a provincial hero, it soon became clear that his student body might turn out to be a serious rival to the government's untested conscript army. The latter force had been somewhat impeded in its development: the government, having first chosen France's army as a model, had suddenly felt obliged to switch over to Germany's when the latter emerged victorious in the war of 1870. The issue on the home front came to a head in 1876, when in order to equip its fledgling troops, the war ministry requisitioned Satsuma's provincial arsenal. Instead of handing it over, Saigo used its contents to equip his own 10,000 followers and started marching them toward Kyoto.

The result was the last, and in many ways the most extraordinary, of all Japan's innumerable civil wars. The question involved was not Saigo's loyalty to the emperor, which had already been amply proven. It was simply whether the imperial, and hence the national, interest would best be served by maintaining the old samurai order as a military caste or by substituting for it a European-style army made up of the sons of peasants, townfolk, and factory workers. Hence it was one instance in which a trial by force of arms was not merely an inevitable, but, in a fashion rarely true of modern military engagements, an entirely functional, procedure.

Superior numbers on the government side eventually resulted in Saigo's retreat to a rocky eminence in his home town, the Satsuma capital of Kagoshima. Here, the samurai army made a suicidal last stand in which practically all of its members fought to the death. Saigo himself, having spent his last afternoon playing a game of Go with one of his captains, committed seppuku in a hillside cave.

The net effect of the Saigo rebellion was to confirm the unity of the nation under imperial power and to accelerate Japan's already rapid advance toward the status of a major world power. What helped most to facilitate this process was the attitude of the emperor toward the families and fellow-clansmen of Saigo's rebels who composed a cross section of the nation. All were treated with complete forbearance

while Saigo himself, with all his previous honors posthumously restored, eventually came to enjoy a niche in Japan's history comparable to that of Robert E. Lee in the history of the United States.

Although an American had been the first to intrude upon Japan's long-preserved privacy, it was not his compatriots who were the most diligent and adroit in following it up. Nor was it the French, who, though they got off to a fast start, made the same error as most of the other foreigners, of supposing that the shogun would continue to be the *de facto* ruler of the country. Among the newcomers, only the British were alert enough to sense what was really going on behind the scenes and to proceed accordingly.

This may have been partly because the British minister, Sir Rutherford Alcock, through previous experience in China, had a better approach to the whole situation. It may also have been partly because of some inherent affinity between the two nations based upon insular characteristics common to both. In any case, what soon became clear was that even such unlikely incidents as the bombardments of Kagoshima and the Choshu forts on Shimonoseki Strait were turning out advantageously for the British in a way that was to have far-reaching consequences for both nations.

The action at Shimonoseki Strait was notable less for the casualties

Delighted by this toy train presented by Admiral Perry, the Japanese quickly completed their own railway line running from Tokyo to Yokohama by 1872.

involved than for the onshore fraternization between Japanese and
British naval officers which followed the shooting. While the French
had been helping the shoguns fortify Edo Bay, the British had concentrated upon developing their contacts among the outer daimyo, especially those of Satsuma, where many of Japan's future leaders under
the Meiji regime were starting their careers. Serving one of the harbor
guns at Kagoshima, when the British squadron put in there to extract
an indemnity for the death of trader Richardson, was a fifteen-year-
old samurai named Heihachiro Togo. Eight years later, he was learning the rudiments of naval warfare on the British training ship
Worcester, at Portsmouth, England.

The lessons about what Britain had accomplished during the years
of Japanese isolation were by no means lost upon the clique of able
samurai who surrounded the boy emperor. While British engineers
were helping Japan build railroads, factories, and an industrial economy, this group was even more interested in developing a navy that
might eventually enable Japanese sea power to become for the Pacific
something like what Britain's had been for the Atlantic. To this end,
dozens of other promising young samurai—most of them naturally
from the maritime province of Satsuma—followed Togo through
naval training in England or, under the guidance of British instruc-
tors, in Japan. Meanwhile, British shipyards took the lead in helping

Japan assemble a fleet that was to meet its first serious test in 1894.

At stake in the Sino-Japanese war was the question of which country was to control the then hopelessly shabby little "hermit kingdom" of Korea. Though long a vassal state of China, Korea now represented to the Japanese a tempting target for colonization along the lines so impressively laid down by its new-found tutor in such matters. As early as 1885, Japan had dispatched a mission to Seoul, modeled on Perry's to Edo, designed to "open" Korea to Japanese trade. This had been followed by a treaty with China under its last Manchu empress whereby each nation promised not to send troops to Korea without advance notice to the other. When, in 1894, the queen of Korea called upon her Manchu colleague in Peking for military assistance in controlling internal disorders attributed to the presence of a Japanese trading colony, the Japanese responded by announcing that they would send in troops as well.

Hostilities started when Togo, as captain of a Japanese cruiser called the *Naniwa,* sank a merchant ship carrying a Chinese regiment to the Korean port of Chemulpo. The conflict ended a year later, with China's capitulation on terms that gave Japan a free hand in Korea, possession of Taiwan, and a $25,000,000 indemnity. However, along with all this, Japan felt that she had also established a claim to the Liaotung Peninsula, where Russia had it in mind to turn the ice-free harbor of Port Arthur into a major naval base. The main result of Japan's smashing victory over the biggest nation in Asia was thus to bring her into abrupt collision with a far more dangerous adversary than the one she had just defeated.

As if the odds in this confrontation were not already long enough, Russia was backed by France and Germany—for both of these were almost equally perturbed by the celerity with which Japan had picked up the knack of Asiatic colonization, long considered a European monopoly. Here once more the affinity between the island empire off the coast of Asia and its counterpart off the coast of Europe came into important play. England and Japan formed an alliance whereby, if either were to become involved in hostilities against more than one opponent, the other would come to her assistance. Since neither Germany nor France was likely to risk a world war to aid Russia, this assured Japan that, if she were to fight her huge neighbor, they would remain on the sidelines. With her hand thus strengthened, she set about trying to adjust the dispute by diplomatic means on the one hand while building up an even more formidable fleet on the other.

Boiled down to essentials, Japan's diplomatic overtures comprised relinquishing her claim to Liaotung, including Port Arthur, and offering her rival exclusive development rights in Manchuria in return for the equivalent in Korea. When, instead, the tsar's government not only ignored these offers but undertook to start a lumber company on the Korean side of the Yalu River, it became apparent that Japan would either have to back down completely, or fight. This time, hostilities started in February of 1904, with a Japanese surprise attack on the Russian base at Port Arthur.

In years to come, much was to be said about the similarity between Japan's opening gambit at Port Arthur and her surprise attack on Pearl Harbor in December, 1941. Perhaps even more noteworthy than its resemblance to the action at Pearl Harbor which was to follow it thirty-seven years later, was its similarity to another naval engagement that had preceded it by more than a hundred. This was Admiral Horatio Nelson's famous surprise assault on the Danish fleet at Copenhagen which—although, like Port Arthur and Pearl Harbor, it preceded any declaration of war—had always been held in the highest esteem by naval authorities in Britain and elsewhere. Schooled for three years aboard a training ship within sight of Nelson's old flagship at Portsmouth, Togo, now Japan's naval commander in chief, had studied the British hero's career with worshipful devotion. His victory at Port Arthur was by no means the only one in which he was to pay Nelson the tribute of imitation, but it was the first that aroused international applause, especially in England where the *Times* hailed it as an act of "daring" and "vigour" which did "high honour to the navy of our gallant allies."

In any case, the obvious points of resemblance between Port Arthur and Pearl Harbor—that both these attacks also preceded a declaration of war—was perhaps less important than two others which have more frequently been overlooked. In both cases Japan felt, not without reason, that her adversary was pretending to offer a diplomatic compromise in order to buy the time that would provide an important strategic advantage. And in both cases time was the most essential element to be considered in the Japanese plan for the war as a whole.

In 1904 the war plan was based on Japan's awareness that Russia was building a battle fleet which, if it were allowed time to join forces with the Russian Far East squadron already based at Port Arthur, would form a combination strong enough to ensure command of the Sea of Japan. This in turn would preclude the possibility of sending Japanese troops to the mainland and thus all chance of winning the war. If, on the other hand, Japan could first knock out the Russian Far East squadron at its home base and then use her own command of the sea to ferry an army to the mainland, she might well be able to capture Port Arthur and hold it against any Russian reinforcements that might reach the scene later.

As things turned out, the attack on Port Arthur, while less successful than its World War II replay, served to enable a Japanese army under General Maresuke Nogi to take Port Arthur by the end of the year. Meanwhile, at the entrance of Tsushima Strait, Togo was lying in wait for the Baltic Fleet which Russia had at last sent to the rescue. The outcome of their encounter would clearly decide that of the war.

Before his greatest victory, at Trafalgar in 1805, Admiral Nelson had signaled to his fleet the message that "England expects that every man will do his duty." Togo had devised a similar message for his fleet to be conveyed by a signal flag representing the letter "Z," pronounced "Zetto," in emulation of the English "Zed" and used as an ideograph meaning "The fate of the nation rests on this single battle. Let every man do his utmost." After weeks of anxious waiting, the Zed flag finally shot up the yardarm of his flagship, *Mikasa,* at 1:45 P.M. on May 27 in Trafalgar's centennial year of 1905. The Russian Fleet had been spotted early that morning at the entrance to the strait, Togo had come out of his lair to meet it, and now, on a windy spring afternoon, the first shots were about to be fired.

Like the Chinese, whose scornful phrase for their Japanese neighbors was "the island dwarfs," the Russians had from the start found it difficult to take their enemies seriously. When the war began, Russian residents of Vladivostok, Mukden, and Port Arthur had entertained the view that the Japanese were as harmless as butterflies, and the fashionable witticism was, "We'll pin one on a postcard and send him home for a souvenir." Now, to be sure, the circumstances had

changed considerably, but still, aboard the Russian ships, the officers and men were confident and in high spirits. Their eight-month voyage around the Cape of Good Hope and through the Straits of Malacca had been an unprecedented feat of navigation. Its successful completion, now all but accomplished, had made them feel ready to take on whatever Japan could send out to stop them. The first shot of the battle, which tore off the wireless aerial on Togo's flagship as it turned sharply at the head of his line of battle, added to their confidence.

While most of the civilized world was waiting eagerly to learn the outcome of the engagement, the only person who in fact had an unobstructed view of it was a thirteen-year-old boy named Sato Ichisaburo perched on the limb of a pine tree on the side of a high hill on the tiny islet of Okinoshima, ten miles off the coast of Kyushu on the east side of the channel. From this unique vantage point, he later reported: "Two rows of scores of warships . . . looked as neat as two rows of go-stones. I never thought that warships looked so beautiful

After long years of isolation Japan showed a willingness to engage again in foreign trade by such diplomatic overtures as the presentation of silk goods.

in the midst of a battle. . . . As [the shells] fell into the sea, they turned into hundreds of water-columns. The guns flashed like lightning and roared like a thousand thunder storms."

Presently the smoke of the guns mixed with the black smoke from the stacks and the slight haze over the water to form a dark cloud that obscured this idyllic picture. What took place under this cloud was a classic demonstration of naval tactics which started with the two fleets, each composed of twelve major warships, steaming along toward the northeast in parallel line-ahead formation while blazing away at each other with all their guns. The Russian ships outweighed Togo's and had more long-range fire power, but every other advantage rested with the Japanese, including speed, marksmanship, and position. Firing with both the wind and the sun at their backs, they had sunk the first of the many Russian battleships that would go down that day by 3:30 P.M. The spectacle of the *Oslyabya* dropping out of action in flames and then turning turtle, with her crew clinging to her sides and rigging, was clearly visible to all the ships behind her in the line of battle as they caught up and passed. In it, they saw their own doom.

In such battleship duels, accepted tactics called for the faster of the two fleets to attempt to "cross the T" of its adversary's line of battle, thus putting the latter in a position from which the guns of all but his leading ship were blocked or "masked" by the ships ahead. As Togo's faster line drew ahead, while simultaneously shortening the range so as to equalize his deficiency in fire power, the Russians, in order to prevent him from getting far enough ahead to turn across the course of their leading ship, were forced to curve away and then try to double back around the rear of the Japanese line. Neither maneuver worked; and by the time the sun went down, three more of their battleships had been sunk, including the flagship, *Suvorov,* from which their wounded commander in chief had been removed to a destroyer.

During the darkness, Japanese cruisers and destroyers worked further havoc. Remnants of the battleship division that had remained afloat during the night were surrounded and forced to surrender the next morning, a hundred miles farther north. Of the more than fifty vessels which had originally set out from the Baltic, only three—a light cruiser and two destroyers—finally reached a haven at Vladivostok.

According to naval statisticians the Battle of Tsushima was the greatest victory in the history of sea warfare and perhaps—since most major subsequent naval engagements have been in large part fought in the air—the greatest that ever will be fought. Japan's fleet under Togo had eventually sunk six out of the eight Russian battleships, captured the remaining two, and sunk, captured, or driven into internment practically all his other warships—and done this at the total cost to Japan of three torpedo boats. The casualty figures were equally one-sided: for Russia almost five thousand men killed and six thousand taken prisoner, against a loss for Japan of 117 killed.

Far more significant than the mere figures were the imponderable results of the victory for the Far East generally and for Japan in particular. Prior to Tsushima, Japan had been an engaging oddity among the world's nations, an exotic museum piece of quaint Oriental feudalism. Thereafter, she was a major world power by any measure—and by far the leading power among the nations of Asia. More than that, by so decisively defeating the world's biggest nation, tiny Japan had shown Asia as well as Europe that there was no qualitative difference between Europeans and Asians—or that, if there were, the superiority might well belong to the latter. Singlehanded, and in the space of a few hours, Japan had in effect ended the colonial era.

At the peace conference in Portsmouth, New Hampshire, arranged by President Theodore Roosevelt the following August, Japan got half of Sakhalin Island, certain development rights in Manchuria, and effective control of Korea. By 1910, two years before Emperor Meiji's death, she had officially annexed that unhappy kingdom and set forth on the course of empire building that would lead eventually to World War II. However, had it been possible for some astronaut to view the future panorama of history as clearly as Sato Ichisaburo had seen the start of the Battle of Tsushima, it would have been clear that, from the Japanese viewpoint, the most important figure of the entire war would prove to have been not Nogi, the victor at Port Arthur, nor Togo, the architect of Tsushima, nor even the great Meiji himself. It was a 22-year-old American second lieutenant who chanced to be present for a single afternoon at the siege of Mukden as a subordinate aide attached to the staff of the U.S. general, who was his father. The second lieutenant's name was Douglas MacArthur.

CHAPTER VI

"I CAN BABY
THEM ALONG"

Among the numerous Japanese family names that often give foreigners trouble, one of the most perplexing is Yamamoto. At the Battle of Tsushima, for example, dozens of Yamamotos were involved and at least three had important roles. One was a wireless expert whose skilled appropriation of Marconi's invention enabled the Japanese to be the first to make advantageous use of it in warfare. Another was Isoroku Yamamoto, later to be commander in chief of the Japanese Navy in World War II, who lost two fingers of his left hand in a gunnery mishap while serving as an ensign on the battleship *Nisshin.* The third and possibly most prestigious of all was Admiral Gombei Yamamoto who, as navy minister in 1904, had given his onetime shipmate, Togo, the job of commander in chief and supported him loyally throughout the war.

When hostilities ended with the Portsmouth Peace Conference, what followed for Togo was a triumphal world tour in the course of which he paid a courtesy call on Theodore Roosevelt at Sagamore Hill. There he gave his host a lesson in how to clean and care for the samurai sword which T.R., by then ex-president, had acquired as a

Sumo *wrestlers perform an extensive ritual before their brief and brutal match.*

souvenir from Emperor Meiji. When Meiji died in 1912, Togo withdrew into glorious retirement which lasted until his death in 1934. Gombei Yamamoto, however, progressed in public life, becoming prime minister in 1913 and again in the late summer of 1923. On the afternoon of September 1 in that year he was in the process of trying to form his new cabinet in a room on the second floor of the Navy Club in Tokyo when, at two minutes before noon, the room suddenly began to sway from side to side and bounce up and down. This was the start of the *Kanto Daishinsai,* or Great Kanto Earthquake Disaster, possibly the most destructive natural catastrophe in human history, in which 144,000 people were to lose their lives within the next forty-eight hours.

Earthquakes in Japan are by no means unusual. Quakes of sufficient intensity to rattle dishes occur several times a month and really major ones at intervals of a few decades. This one, however, was clearly something exceptional, even among the latter. It lasted for only fifteen seconds, but its severity was such that, as the admiral made his way toward the stairway, chunks of plaster falling from the ceiling severely bruised his left arm. Brushing debris off his sleeve as he came down the stairs, he said to the reporters who were waiting to hear the names he had on his list: "Well, you will certainly have plenty to write about today."

This was putting it mildly. As measured on the widely accepted Richter Scale for measuring such phenomena, the Kanto earthquake of 1923 rated 8.3, or about the same as the San Francisco one of 1906—in which, however, the death toll was a mere 1,500. The extent of destruction caused by a major quake usually depends less on the Richter rating, which measures intensity at the quake's surface focal point, or epicenter, than on other circumstances, including the proximity of this point to major cities. The epicenter of the Kanto quake was about thirty miles south of Yokohama and fifty miles south of Tokyo, but even more relevant than its location was the time of its occurrence—just when lunch was being cooked over red-hot coals in millions of wooden houses with straw-mat floors, paper windows, and pine-board siding.

Of the 144,000 deaths attributed to the earthquake, fewer than 10,000 were caused by buildings that crashed down, by tidal waves, or

The growth of industry was rapid in Japan. In these 1925 photographs, village women carry porcelain and a man turns a device for weaving straw hats.

by other immediate consequences of the convulsion, such as human beings being swallowed up by the ground itself—a misfortune of which, incidentally, there has never been any authenticated case in any earthquake anywhere. Nor were most of the casualties caused by people being burned alive in the conflagrations that started immediately and reached their maximum intensity a few hours later. The fatalities resulted in most cases from suffocation as a side effect of huge firestorms whose flames whirled hundreds of feet into the air. Such storms—to be duplicated in 1945 as the result of air raids on Tokyo—drew all oxygen away from the ground area beneath them, thus preventing tens of thousands of people from breathing for periods of time long enough to be lethal. One passed across an open area near the Sumida River where some 40,000 terrified city dwellers had huddled together to find refuge from surrounding fires. In the three or four minutes it remained overhead, the storm effected the deaths of almost the entire 40,000.

Vast national calamities like earthquakes, volcanic eruptions, and typhoons are often ignored by serious historians even when the destruction in terms of human life and treasure—in this case the latter amounted to some $2 billion—approximates that of a major war. The causes of such calamities lie outside the range of human control, and their consequences are too widely distributed and too diverse to be accurately appraised. In this instance, however, there were certain results which may be worth noting if only because of their total incongruity both with each other and with the event that gave rise to them.

Among the foreign visitors to Tokyo in the early nineteen hundreds had been a knowledgeable young American architect named Frank Lloyd Wright. Understandably responsive to Japanese styles in aesthetics generally and in residential construction in particular, Wright's own novel ideas about the latter were much influenced by what he saw. On his return to the United States, he became a collector of Japanese prints which he frequently purchased from the Yamanaka Gallery on East Fifty-Seventh Street in New York. Shortly after the death of Emperor Meiji, it occurred to the Japanese government that Tokyo needed an impressive hotel for the convenience of the increasing number of visitors from Europe and the United States. To this end a commission was dispatched on an international tour to scrutinize major hostelries in other capitals and select the architect best equipped to design one for Japan.

Their first stop was New York, where the members of the commission put up at the Plaza Hotel, then the city's newest and best. When they dropped in at the Yamanaka Gallery, which was only two blocks downtown, they naturally sought advice on their quest from its proprietor who responded by introducing his young print-collecting client. The fact that Wright, far from being interested in erecting the sort of monument to traditional taste which the commissioners presumably had in mind, might choose to express his own highly divergent thoughts in such matters in no way diminished their interest in the plans which he presently submitted. Disparities in Western architectural styles, all of them differing far more from any Japanese style than from each other, no doubt remained for Wright's potential clients largely imperceptible.

Wright's arrival in Tokyo was delayed by World War I. When he finally got there in 1921, the progress of his work was retarded by further complications, including the discovery that the site chosen for the new Imperial Hotel was an undrainable swamp lying between the imperial palace and the shore of Tokyo Bay. Ever resourceful, Wright asserted that, by placing his structure on piles sunk far down into the mud, he could not only overcome the handicap provided by the swamp but convert it into an asset, since its very instability would help to cushion the effects of Tokyo's numerous earthquakes. After additional difficulties concerning finances, which arose when Wright's expenditures exceeded his budget by some 200 per cent, the architect returned to the United States leaving his work to be completed by an assistant named Antonín Raymond. Wright, however, remained curious about the fate of his first major international commission. When he saw newspaper headlines which said in effect TOKYO DESTROYED BY EARTHQUAKE, he dispatched an anxious cable to his chief backer, Baron Okura, to ask how the Imperial had weathered the shock.

By a dramatic coincidence, the date of the earthquake was also that which had been chosen for the opening of the Imperial Hotel, where a gala luncheon for distinguished members of the foreign community was scheduled for 12:30 P.M. Final preparations for this were going on at full speed when the earthquake started. Owing largely to the

OVERLEAF: *Japan's beauty knows no season, as seen by the Golden Pavilion in Kyoto, left, and the Garden of Manpukuji Temple, Shimane prefecture, right.*

presence of mind of the hotel manager, a fire in the kitchen caused when a bowl of fat tipped over on an electric stove was speedily extinguished. During the night, when flames from nearby conflagrations approached the hotel, bucket brigades kept the hotel's roof wet until the wind providentially changed shortly after midnight. For several weeks after the quake, the hotel provided emergency accommodations for hundreds of foreign diplomats and businessmen whose houses had been destroyed by fire. As soon as cable service was restored after the disaster, Baron Okura replied to Wright's inquiry with a message of congratulation: HOTEL STANDS UNDAMAGED AS MONUMENT OF YOUR GENIUS HUNDREDS OF HOMELESS PROVIDED FOR BY PERFECTLY MAINTAINED SERVICE CONGRATULATIONS OKURA

Never one to display undue reticence in such matters, Wright speedily convened a press conference at which he said nothing to dissuade reporters from drawing the inference that the Imperial was not only still operating but also that it was the only building in Tokyo that had remained standing through the disaster. This was by no means the case. In fact, hundreds of other solid masonry buildings in both Tokyo and Yokohama also withstood the quake—most notably those of a prolific British architect named Josiah Condor whose numerous commercial structures in Tokyo's nearby Marunouchi district suffered considerably less damage than Wright's. Nonetheless, the Imperial Hotel's thoroughly undeserved fame as the only building that had stood up through the great Tokyo quake was to prove far more unshakable than the edifice itself; and Wright's renown as the man who had designed and built it flourished accordingly. While by no means wholly responsible for the architectural revolution that was to revitalize the world's cities during the next four decades, the world-wide repute of Wright's Imperial Hotel was to facilitate and hasten its progress. By the time this famous edifice was demolished in 1967 to make room for a bigger one, the Kanto earthquake had thus been instrumental in altering not only the appearance of Tokyo but also that of many of the other great cities in the world as well.

Comparable to the impact on architecture of the Kanto earthquake was another indirect consequence of the disaster which had its origins on the floor of the U.S. Senate a year later. In 1923 foreign reaction to news of the disaster was naturally to send aid of every sort, in copious

quantities. Leader in the effort, as the most prosperous country in the
world and Japan's nearest Western neighbor, was quite properly the
United States, whose contributions included sending first the Pacific
Fleet to the scene with food and other emergency supplies and then
monetary benefits totaling over $10,000,000. The Japanese were deeply
impressed by these generosities, and it seemed for a time that, insofar
as such a calamity could have minor compensations, one of them might
well be warmer relations with the Western world generally and with
the United States in particular.

On the contrary, a year later the U.S. Senate was debating an immigration bill whereby, instead of welcoming all comers as had once been
the custom, the United States would impose a ceiling upon new arrivals
of 150,000 per year. Within this total, each nation was to have a quota
proportionate to the number of its nationals already present in America. Had this formula been impartially applied to Japan, the result
would have been an annual influx of only 146, or less than .000001
per cent of the total U.S. population. Since the Japanese already admitted were proving themselves to be model citizens, one might have
supposed that such a modest quota would have been readily accepted
or even, under the special circumstance, enlarged by a decimal or two.
Yet the proposed bill provided that "Asiatics"—in other words, Japanese, since Chinese were already specifically ruled out by another
law—were to be excluded altogether.

Even more astonishing than the bill itself were the tactics employed
to further its passage by Senator Henry Cabot Lodge of Massachusetts, just then fresh from his triumphs in keeping the United States
out of the League of Nations. Seeing that the only practical purpose
of canceling the minute Japanese quota would be to offer a gratuitous
insult to a friendly neighbor, Secretary of State Charles Evans Hughes
requested Japan's ambassador in Washington to write him a personal
letter pointing out what effect he thought the bill would have in Japan.
When the ambassador replied that, by stigmatizing his compatriots as
"unworthy and undesirable," the bill might produce "grave consequences," Lodge, although fully aware of the circumstances under
which the letter had been written, chose to interpret it in the Senate
debate as "unwarranted interference" in U.S. affairs. Aided by this
adroit forensic gambit, the bill was duly enacted into law.

The impact of this uncalled-for slur upon a nation whose ruling house was demonstrably the world's oldest and whose aristocratic traditions antedated New England's somewhat more mercantile ones by well over a thousand years was precisely as foreseen. Its effect was not merely to cancel all the good will established by the wholly spontaneous U.S. reaction to the catastrophe of the year before but to convert Japanese gratitude into resentment of what now appeared to have been insincere and calculated condescension. In due course, the grave consequences of the Lodge amendment became only too apparent. These were to strengthen the already influential element in the Japanese Army high command which believed that their nation's future role in world affairs should be to disregard all protestations of friendship from the West, along with all thought of cooperation with Europe or the U.S., and instead to carve out a Japanese empire on the continent of Asia.

While the U.S. exclusion act of 1924 undoubtedly helped the expansionist clique in the Japanese Army to gain and maintain control of the nation's foreign policy in the ensuing years, this ill-conceived legislation was by no means the only, or even a main, factor

The Tokyo Imperial Hotel designed by Frank Lloyd Wright withstood a terrible earthquake in 1923 only to be demolished in 1967 in the name of progress.

in these developments. Among numerous causes, another more noteworthy one was interservice rivalry between the army and navy.

While it was the Japanese Navy that had received the most acclaim at home as well as abroad for winning the Russo-Japanese War, it was the army that in fact had done most of the fighting and certainly most of the dying. Though nominally joined with the Allies during World War I, Japan had used her participation chiefly as a ticket of admission to the Versailles Peace Conference where, having already gobbled up former German concessions in Tsingtao, she now acquired a protectorate over Germany's former island possessions in the Pacific, including the Marianas, Carolines, and Marshalls. This tended to increase the navy's responsibilities and hence its prestige, as did the outcome of the Washington Naval Conference of 1921. At this meeting, it was agreed that the major naval powers would submit to a ten-year moratorium on capital-ship building and that the United States, England, and Japan would pare their existing fleets down to a 5-5-3 ratio. Ostensibly a plan for limited disarmament, this arrangement in fact licensed Japan as the third strongest naval power in the world.

For Japan, the navy was a relatively recent acquisition, dating back only to the Meiji restoration, whereas land warfare, prior to the Toku-

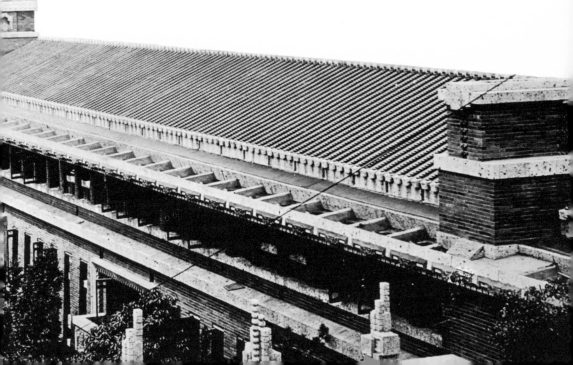

gawa era, had been the nation's major industry and even thereafter, through the durable samurai code of bushido, the most formative influence upon the national character. The navy high command was composed largely of samurai from Satsuma whose seafaring heritage dated back a mere three centuries to the days when the Shimazu warships were the only ones Japan had. The army's regional stronghold was the rival province of Choshu whose military traditions antedated even the wars of the Taira and the Minamoto. However, these deep-rooted geographical and functional sources of sharp interservice rivalry in Japan were by no means the only reason why this rivalry was to have a disproportionate leverage upon national policy.

The navy's achievements had in effect challenged the army to prove itself of equal importance to the national destiny. This challenge was underlined by certain basic disparities between army and navy temperament generally, a factor discernible not only in Japan but often in other nations as well. Seagoing people tend to be inherently adventurous souls who welcome new places, new people, and quite frequently, even new ideas. In naval officers this characteristic is likely to be nurtured by their voyages around the rest of the world, which help them pick up valuable pointers about human nature in general and the capabilities of potential enemies in particular. Army training conversely takes place mostly at home and seems to encourage, or at least to confirm, a more rigid and parochial outlook whereby alien viewpoints are impatiently brushed aside or simply ignored. In Japan during the twenties and thirties, such disparities between army and navy personnel, accentuated by outside circumstances, helped give competition, first between the two services and then between rival factions within the army, a decisive importance.

While the Meiji Constitution promulgated by the emperor in 1889 provided for a bicameral Diet, this body, prior to the 1920s, had never exerted an influence commensurate with that of parliamentary institutions in Great Britain or the United States. In Japan actual power had resided in a cabinet composed, during the later years of the Meiji era, of worthy successors to the able young samurai advisers who had counseled the emperor at the beginning of his reign. Of even the more recent Meiji dignitaries, however, only a few had survived their ruler, and by the mid-twenties, the only one of the so-called *genro,* or elder statesmen, who remained was the venerable Prince Saionji who lived on through the thirties. Meanwhile, the old emperor himself had been succeeded by an unreliable son whose antic attitude toward his largely ceremonial duties sometimes led to alarming innovations in governmental procedures. On one famous occasion, when handed a parchment scroll from which to read off a message to the Diet, he amused himself instead by rolling it up into a make-believe telescope through which he peered playfully about the chamber.

In 1921, two years before the earthquake, Emperor Taisho's obvious unsuitability for office made it necessary to appoint as regent his son, Hirohito, the latter whose reign name was to be Showa. Hirohito was a well-meaning and intelligent young man who, however, also lacked most of Emperor Meiji's enthusiasm and aptitude for rule. Under the tutelage of Admiral Togo, he had responded to his mentor's nautical bias by developing an intense interest in, not the navy, but marine biology. In this field, he achieved scholarly distinction which, however, did little to compensate for his disinterest in terrestrial politics.

One of the conclusions drawn by Japan from the victory of the Allies in World War I was that democracy was a stronger and hence more desirable form of government than autocracy, as represented by the Central Powers. The result was a sudden lurch toward truly representative government accomplished during the early twenties through bills providing first for wider, and then, in 1925, for universal, male suffrage. However, while this made it seem possible that Japan's Diet would eventually move into the power vacuum created by the demise of Meiji and the genro, the Constitution contained at least two weaknesses which effectively precluded this possibility.

One weakness was that, while the Diet had the right to endorse or reject the budgets presented by the Cabinet, it did not have the right to substitute a new one of its own. This meant that, in the event of rejection, the budget of the previous year would remain operative. Since the main outlay was usually for the armed forces, this gave the military a disproportionate hold on the nation's purse strings.

The second weakness was that, while the emperor was the constitutional source of all power in the state, both armed services as well as the Diet itself were considered to be equally, and independently, representative of that power. Hence, if the army took an action not approved by the Diet, it could and, as things turned out, frequently did, claim to be acting on an interpretation of the emperor's wishes quite as valid as any that could be supplied by mere politicians. An emperor like Hirohito's grandfather might, to be sure, have clarified his wishes so emphatically as to remove all doubts about their interpretation, but such a course would have been wholly out of character for Hirohito.

During the early twenties, and even after the initiation of universal male suffrage, numerous superficial clues suggested that despite these constitutional flaws, Japan might well be on the threshold of genuine Western style democracy. Western games like tennis, golf, and even American baseball became widely popular. Social customs changed enough to allow women to work in offices or, for that matter, as hostesses in dance halls or waitresses in Western-style restaurants. Western dress became increasingly popular, along with Western movies, music, and architecture—especially in Tokyo where massive steel and concrete buildings replaced wooden structures in wide areas destroyed by the post-earthquake fires. What was more to the point was that all these perhaps superficial indices had a solid economic substructure.

During the Meiji period, Japan's financial and commercial community had developed rapidly and along peculiarly Japanese lines, in which family connections and clan loyalties were closely interwoven. Most typically Japanese of the evolving commercial institutions were naturally the biggest and most influential—the huge corporate structures called *zaibatsu* which, by the second decade of the twentieth century, had come to dominate the business scene in a fashion unparalleled in the West by even the biggest corporate giants. Each of the four major combines—Mitsui, Mitsubishi, Sumitomo, and Yasuda— while controlled by a single family, comprised thousands of employees. Each was involved in dozens of separate but interrelated enterprises, rather like what are nowadays known in the United States as "conglomerates" except that in Japan the conglomerations were even more heterogeneous.

The political influence of the zaibatsu upon the two major political parties, through friendly and familial relations with the Diet and the Cabinet, was naturally substantial. However, the essential point was not so much that one party might be inclined to favor the interests of the Mitsui while the other favored those of the Mitsubishi. Rather it was that all of the zaibatsu—and with them most of the important banks and the business community as a whole—were increasingly disposed to view the Diet rather than the armed forces as the institution most capable of directing the affairs of the nation.

During the twenties, Japan's business leaders had become increasingly inclined to doubt the pre-World War I theory, still held by the military, that what Japan needed was a colonial empire in China as a source of raw materials and a captive market for the products to be made out of them. Surely it would be far less costly, and far less provoking to valued clients in the Western world, simply to buy raw materials and then build up a world-wide export trade based on Japan's capacity to manufacture goods more cheaply than the West could. And if it were really possible for Japan thus to achieve economic security by peaceful means, why go to all the trouble and expense of conquest?

Themselves a relatively new force in the nation, Japan's business leaders were by no means eager to surrender their recently acquired status and influence to the military, especially the army with its enthusiasm for huge expenditures for armaments and its priority claims upon the labor force. All in all, as big business became more and more integrated with the political establishment, it began to seem entirely conceivable that Japan would be able to prosper by peaceful means despite a burgeoning population that, already well over sixty million, was still growing at the rate of one million a year.

What prevented the realization of this happy outcome was primarily the onset of the Great Depression which, in Japan, was superimposed on a domestic slump that had started in 1927. Hurt first by the reduced buying power of her foreign clients and then by protective tariffs imposed by them upon her products, Japan lacked the natural resources that gave most Western nations, and especially the United States, the self-sufficiency to ride out the storm. As the thirties began, the consensus of the business community in general and eventually even that of the zaibatsu veered back to the thesis underlying her territorial expansion before and during World War I, to which the army leaders had adhered throughout.

An additional factor in the equation now, and one which derived

new weight from the onset of the Depression, was the threat of Communism as embodied by the U.S.S.R. Always suspicious of Russia—and, during the imperial era, not without good cause—Japan was now especially alert to conditions in China where Chiang Kai-shek was fighting a loose coalition of unpredictable war lords on the one hand and Mao Tse-tung's Communist forces on the other. The threat of a Communist take-over in China which would menace Japan's interests in Korea helped accelerate the shifting balance of political forces within Japan and the change in Japanese policy that derived from it.

The first substantive results of this profound change came in September of 1931, when Japanese army units stationed in Manchuria ostensibly to safeguard the South Manchurian Railway which Japan had acquired from Russia a quarter of a century before, suddenly felt themselves obliged to take over the entire area comprising some 400,-000 square miles and a population of some 30 million. While they apparently did so without the knowledge, let alone the approval, of their government, what was even more indicative of the new sentiment in Japan was that neither the army high command nor the government saw fit to rescind the occupation or even to rebuke the unit commanders concerned. Instead, they endorsed the take-overs the following year by providing Manchuria with the new name of Manchukuo and a young puppet emperor in the person of Henry Pu-yi, heir to the Manchu dynasty that had been ousted from Peking by the revolution of 1911.

Japanese immigrants to California enjoy high spirits in this 1918 photograph.

One result of this feat was to give Japan a major overseas source of raw materials. Another—since the feat had been accomplished at negligible human or monetary cost—was widespread acceptance of the army as the true warden of national welfare. When the League of Nations denounced the action and withheld recognition of the new state, Japan responded by blandly withdrawing from that august organization. Protests from the United States—whose stand on tariffs and immigration were hardly calculated to have ensured a sympathetic hearing on such matters—were likewise politely ignored.

After what Japan was thereafter to refer to as "the Manchurian Incident," the question was not whether Japan was to have a two-party system of parliamentary government, much less which of the two parties was to win election. It was merely which one of the two contending factions in the army was to determine the destiny of the nation. And this question was to be decided, not by the ballot box, but by a series of assassinations, mutinies, and executions culminating in the unsuccessful coup of February 26, 1936. In this, a group of young officers attempted to take over the national government by murdering all its leading figures. Among those whom they meant to include but who more or less miraculously survived were the prime minister, who was a retired admiral named Keisuke Okada; the emperor's grand chamberlain, who was another retired admiral, named Kantaro Suzuki; and the venerable Prince Saionji.

The instigators of the coup belonged to an army faction known as the "Imperial Way" group, composed of young officers who believed that Japan's expansionist trend had gone far enough and should come to an end with the development of Manchukuo. Their opponents within the army, known as the "Control" group, were mostly senior officers who favored further expansion into China itself, as a means of preventing the spread of Communism as well as of enhancing Japanese prosperity. When the coup leaders were executed by firing squad, the expansionist faction acquired control not only of the army but of the government itself through the high command's long-established veto on the selection of a war minister. This in effect included a veto over the selection of the entire Cabinet since, if it found any members unacceptable, the high command could simply refrain from endorsing a war minister until others more to its liking were substituted. Thus, under a subsequent succession of compliant prime ministers, the army control group was able to impose first a rigid press censorship and then nationwide surveillance by a species of secret police, charged with maintaining "thought control." Meanwhile, with Manchukuo well in hand, the next step in overseas expansion took place in July, 1937.

This time the move was not the result of independent action on the part of a subordinate army unit in the field but rather the response of the duly constituted government in Tokyo to a genuine crisis in China. When a Japanese unit assigned to duty in an area near Peking was fired upon in the dark of a July evening by Chinese soldiers whose identity was never clearly established, the result was a skirmish which, according to subsequent evidence, was prolonged by Communist elements in the hope of involving Chiang and the Japanese in outright war. If so, the hope was amply justified. After efforts to negotiate a truce in the field had failed, Tokyo headquarters authorized the local commander to "launch a punitive expedition against the Chinese troops who have been taking action derogatory to the prestige of the Empire of Japan."

The Japanese punitive expedition, whose activities had originally been scheduled to last for three months, began by seizing Peking and Tientsin, taking over most of northern China, and in December capturing the capital at Nanking. Chiang Kai-shek retreated first to Hankow and then, when the Japanese pushed on and took that city in the fall of 1938, to the more remote and better protected stronghold of Chungking. With much of China already more or less under control, the Japanese armies settled down to wait him out. They were still doing so when World War II broke out in Europe in September of 1939, thus putting a new face on the situation.

That the inhabitants of Japan and the United States, as the vanguards of the eastward- and westward-moving currents of humanity, would eventually collide, peacefully or otherwise, had of course been inevitable from the moment in prehistory when their divergent migrations started. Temporarily deferred when each reached the shores of the world's biggest ocean, the collision had been further postponed first by Japan's seclusion policy and then by America's preoccupation

with domestic expansion. By 1941, however, these barriers were no
longer effective and the time had now finally arrived for the major confrontation to which Perry's visitation and the subsequent decades of
trade and diplomatic relations had been merely the prelude. As was
perhaps equally inevitable, the confrontation began with a diplomatic
colloquy which, for consistent confusion and mutual misapprehension,
may well have set some sort of record.

Protagonists in the colloquy were two heads of state whose back-
grounds might at first glance have seemed conducive to mutual understanding. Japan's prime minister by this time was Prince Fumimaro
Konoye who, in 1940, had been persuaded to take the post, despite his
personal misgivings, by the argument that no one else could restrain
the army from a course which most of Japan's ablest nonmilitary
leaders believed would lead to disaster. A descendant of the Fujiwara,
a protégé of Prince Saionji, and perhaps the closest friend of the emperor, Prince Konoye was prepared to do all in his power to reach an
understanding with the United States—but his power was severely
limited.

As Konoye's opposite number in America, Franklin Roosevelt had
the advantage of a comparably patrician lineage which, while much
shorter and wholly devoid of deities, at least went back to the Dutch
patroons and included his Japanophile cousin and predecessor in the
White House, Theodore Roosevelt. F.D.R.'s liabilities were an extremely hazy knowledge of the Far East and the fact that he had what
seemed to him to be much more pressing problems on his mind, such
as the war in Europe. However, what was much more relevant than
any potential congeniality between the principals involved, since they
were never to meet, was the sorry inability of their chief spokesmen
to cope with, or even to comprehend, the true issues at stake.

For the U.S., the major figure involved was Secretary of State Cor-
dell Hull, a solemn and well-meaning ex-senator whose seasoning
as a Tennessee politician, while commendably thorough, was scarcely
the ideal preparation for unraveling the complexities of the crisis now
confronting his nation in the Orient. While well aware of his own
limitations in this respect, Secretary Hull did little to diminish them
by his choice of a departmental adviser. This was Stanley Hornbeck,
an "old China hand," whose partiality to his favorite section of the

Far East gave him, like most Sinologues of the period, an almost psychopathic distrust of Japan which extended even to the able and industrious U.S. ambassador in Tokyo, Joseph C. Grew.

Even more discouraging in their way than those of the American representatives were the shortcomings of the chief spokesman for Prince Konoye, since, while the prime minister took a more direct part in the colloquy than F.D.R., he was nine thousand miles away from Washington. This was Japan's one-eyed Ambassador Admiral Kichisaburo Nomura, later to be portrayed in American propaganda of the period as the wily and deceitful villain of the drama. In fact, Nomura was a bluff old sea dog whose liking for the United States, while entirely sincere, was hardly an adequate substitute for ordinary diplomatic finesse, let alone the superhuman skills that would have been required to justify Japan's aggression in China.

The issue which these unlikely participants sat down to discuss in the summer of 1941 was one which might well have taxed a much more congenial group of much more talented specialists. By this time, Japan's militarists had signed both a nonaggression pact with the Soviet Union and a tripartite pact with Germany and Italy. The latter agreement guaranteed Japan's allegiance to the Axis Powers in the event of U.S. entry into the European war, in return for their endorsement of her primacy in Asia. Thus emboldened to go forward with plans for what was termed a "Greater East Asia Co-Prosperity Sphere," Japan had negotiated an arrangement with Vichy France which allowed her to send troops into what was then French Indochina. The purpose of this move was ostensibly to facilitate the subjugation of Chiang Kai-shek, but it also constituted an obvious threat to Malaya, Singapore, and the Dutch East Indies. The prompt reaction of the United States, in which Holland and Great Britain soon concurred, was to impose an embargo on exports to Japan.

Japan's war machine depended on imports of oil and rubber, of which her on-hand reserves were sufficient for, at the most, two years. By depriving her of both these necessities, the embargo appeared to present a choice of two alternatives, neither of which held much appeal. One was to knuckle under completely to the ABCD powers (American, British, Chinese, and Dutch) by forgetting about the Co-Prosperity Sphere completely and retiring from China, on the somewhat dubious assumption that her docility would then be rewarded by handouts adequate to keep her population alive. The other was an immediate all-out effort to conquer the whole of Southeast Asia while she still had the means of doing so and while A, B, and D were still preoccupied in Europe. If victorious, Japan would thus gain assured supplies of oil, rubber, and everything else she might ever need on her own account—but what she could by no means be assured of was the victory.

Faced with this choice, Japan's militarists were understandably inclined to accept the second alternative, although even they were well aware of the desperate risks involved. Her more judicious statesmen, including the prime minister and even, to the extent that he could grasp the implications of the dilemma, the emperor, were inclined to try to find some compromise. Their hope was that the U.S. would rescind the embargo if Japan would agree eventually to withdraw to some extent from China without giving up her previously established claims in Manchukuo and Korea. Under these conditions, both militarists and moderates in Japan concurred that their best course would be to try to reach some sort of compromise with the U.S. while at the same time preparing to take the gamble on war if no compromise were reached. A cutoff date for negotiations was originally set for the end of October.

To suggest that, in planning for war while at the same time engaging in diplomatic negotiations with the United States during the summer and fall of 1941, Japan was guilty of some kind of shocking duplicity is, of course, utter nonsense. All nations, including the United States—which maintains both a State Department and a Department of Defense for precisely that reason—do essentially the same thing most of the time. What is more pertinent is that, in the case of Japan, simultaneous activities on both levels were carried to characteristically extreme lengths, and that the U.S. was only too well aware of the fact.

U.S. awareness of Japan's preparations for war was due to amazingly ingenious efforts on the part of its cryptographers, whereby the State Department as well as the army and navy had become privy to practically all coded Japanese messages. However far from assisting Washington diplomats, their ability to read Japanese cyphers may actually have been a liability in disguise for two reasons. One reason was that, in putting messages into English for the perusal of State

Department officers, cryptographers and translators were often inclined, subconsciously or otherwise, to shade their meaning in the way that would be most acceptable, and hence most intelligible, to their superiors. Another was that the detailed knowledge of Japan's war planning inevitably gave her simultaneous efforts in the diplomatic field the appearance of being merely a cover and thus made it easier to reject them as wholly insincere.

The talks in Washington had actually started well before Japan's dispatch of troops to Indochina which took place in July, shortly after Hitler's attack on Russia. The basis on which they were to be conducted had been stated in one of the early meetings between Nomura and Hull at the latter's apartment on April 14. Hull's opening gambit was an introductory speech which, in somewhat truncated form, ran as follows:

"The one paramount preliminary question about which my government is concerned is a definite assurance in advance that the Japanese Government has the willingness and ability to go forward with a plan . . . in relation to the problems of a settlement; to abandon its present doctrine of military conquest by force and . . . adopt the principles which this government has been proclaiming and practicing as embodying the foundation on which all relations between nations should properly rest."

He then handed Nomura a sheet of paper on which these principles, proclaimed and practiced as embodying a foundation, were defined in almost equally Latinate terms, to wit:

1. Respect for the territorial integrity and the sovereignty of each and all nations.

2. Support of the principle of noninterference in the internal affairs of other countries.

3. Support of the principle of equality, including equality of commercial opportunity.

4. Nondisturbance of the status quo in the Pacific except as the status quo may be altered by peaceful means.

While the principles themselves were comparatively intelligible, though certainly susceptible to varying interpretations, they made little apparent impression on Nomura—possibly because Hull's introduction, uttered in his characteristic Tennessee twang, had already far exceeded his auditor's comprehension. The ambassador therefore committed a diplomatic error even more grave than that of Hull in using language of self-defeating complexity. This was to omit even sending the four principles, to which Hull attached vast importance, to his government in Tokyo.

Early in August, President Roosevelt left Washington for a meeting with Winston Churchill on the *Prince of Wales* off Newfoundland, where they drafted stern messages to be sent to Japan from both Washington and London. When it developed that time was needed to strengthen the fortifications of Singapore against attack by land, F.D.R. remained confident. "Leave that to me," he said, "I think I can baby them along for three months." However, on his return to Washington, F.D.R. found a new element in the situation in the form of a suggestion from Prince Konoye that he and the president have an immediate meeting to discuss the whole situation. The invitation was followed by an official proposal offering to withdraw all Japanese troops from Indochina as soon as peace could be made with China, and promising to make no further advances into neighboring countries. As to Hull's four principles, which had by this time arrived in Tokyo as part of an official U.S. missive, these were "the prime requisites of a true peace and should be applied not only in the Pacific but throughout the world."

In a jovial mood on his return from the summit meeting with Churchill, F.D.R.'s immediate reaction to Prince Konoye's suggestion for a prompt sequel to it was enthusiastic. He informally suggested that Juneau, Alaska, and mid-October might be an appropriate time and place. Eventually, however, nothing came of the proposal, largely because Hull thought it had the "hand-to-heart touch" of Hitler at Munich while Stanley Hornbeck thought it useless unless Japan agreed in advance to considerably more specific compliance with U.S. demands. Despite the urgings from Tokyo of Ambassador Grew, F.D.R. heeded Hornbeck and Hull.

By now it was the beginning of October. The Japanese, not without cause, had reached the conclusion that the U.S. was less interested in reaching a solution than in using the negotiations simply to buy time— during which Japan's limited oil reserves were being used up at the rate of 12,000 tons a day. Pressed into postponing the October deadline, the army had now set December 1 as the date on which, if the Washington talks had not produced any tangible results, the die would be cast for war. Under these conditions, what Japan considered her last possible concession was transmitted by Nomura and Saburo Kurusu— a professional career diplomat sent over to aid the former in the last crucial weeks of negotiation—on November 20. This proposal—mistranslated in the message that reached Hull as an "ultimatum"—was for a *"modus vivendi"* to take effect pending a final solution. It called for an immediate withdrawal of Japanese troops from southern Indochina and eventual withdrawal of all troops from China itself in return for which the United States would sell Japan a million tons of aviation gasoline. The proposal found its way to F.D.R. himself, who was sufficiently impressed to scribble out a *modus vivendi* of his own to be offered in reply. In this he proposed to offer Japan "some oil and rice now—more later" in return for agreement "not to invoke the tripartite alliance even if U.S. gets into European war" and "not to send additional troops to Indochina, Manchurian border or any place South." Meanwhile the U.S. would "introduce Japs to Chinese to talk things over."

By way of answering the Japanese proposal, Hull proceeded first to have the F.D.R. memorandum worked up into a formal State Department document and then to submit it to the other nations concerned— China, Britain, and Holland. After all this had been attended to, and after all three had found various defects in it which required modifications making it less acceptable to Japan, Japan's deadline, once more postponed to December 7, was almost at hand. Hull now decided that the F.D.R. memorandum as amended was not really worth sending and decided instead to answer Japan's proposal with a suggested program of his own which his assistants thereupon set about putting into draft form. When this reached Japan—Konoye had meanwhile been replaced as prime minister by General Hideki Tojo—it turned out to be in effect a restatement of a plan, calling for immediate and total withdrawal from China, which Japan had turned down the previous June. What it elicited from Tokyo was the lengthy declaration of war which reached Nomura on the evening of December 6 and which his staff—several members of which had spent the preceding evening at an office party—was still struggling to put into English when the Jap-

anese planes began to drop their bombs on Pearl Harbor at 7 A.M.
Hawaiian time the next morning.

Of the events and negotiations leading up to Pearl Harbor, the clearest and most objective account so far available in English is that provided by historian John Toland in his superlative study of the Pacific war, *The Rising Sun*. According to Toland, a conciliatory answer to Japan's final proposal would almost undoubtedly have brought about either Japanese agreement or else enough debate in Tokyo to have forced further postponement of the war deadline. Such a delay would have made an attack on Pearl Harbor before the spring of 1942 impractical because of weather conditions. By then the situation in Europe would have changed enough to have caused Japan to reconsider risking her destiny with that of the Axis Powers.

However, while it may well be that war between the United States and Japan could have been avoided if each had understood the other's position, much the same sort of thing might be said about many other wars; and the muddled nature of efforts upon both sides to reach a diplomatic compromise in 1941 was less the exception than the rule in such matters. Like most other forms of human altercations, wars result, very often if not usually, less from any evil intention on the part of either side than simply from certain deep-seated deficiencies in the human capacity for communication as so far developed. The negotiations between the United States and Japan in 1941 were merely an unusually flagrant and conspicuous case in point.

CHAPTER VII

THE
SLEEPING
GIANT

Among the limitless hypotheses advanced to account for Japanese oddities of behavior, some of the more ingenious are those which were proffered by the noted British sociologist-anthropologist Geoffrey Gorer, when he was attached to a top secret psychological warfare unit in Washington, D.C., during World War II. One of Gorer's findings was that breast feeding of Japanese children is often prolonged to an age at which the recipient would much prefer more solid nutriment. Gorer drew the conclusion that this procedure helps account for such idiosyncrasies among the Japanese as their emphasis on the appearance rather than the flavor of food, their apparent prejudice against low, even numbers, and their widespread distaste for symmetry as a virtue in art and architecture.

For understandable reasons, Gorer's somewhat recondite theories about Nipponese child rearing brought him few accolades from high-ranking officers in the U.S. armed forces. Nonetheless, top admirals to the contrary notwithstanding, the possibility that at least one of Gorer's theories may have had noteworthy relevance to the actualities of naval warfare may be suggested by the following passage in B. H. Liddell

Modern warriors, heirs to Japan's ancient military class, on the eve of the Second World War.

Hart's authoritative *History of the Second World War,* dealing with the surprise attack on Pearl Harbor:

"The Japanese also benefited from the use of what has been called the 'unequal leg' attack. Approaching in darkness, the carriers launched their planes at first light when at the nearest point to the target, then turned away from the target but not on a directly reversed route, and were joined by their aircraft at a point farther from the target than when they had been launched. Thus the Japanese aircraft flew one short, and one long, leg—whereas pursuing American aircraft would have to fly two long legs, one out and one back. That disadvantage had not been considered by the American defense planners."

The necessity for flying two long legs in pursuit of Japanese planes at Pearl Harbor—which in effect greatly diminished any possibility that U.S. bombers could retaliate for the surprise attack—was by no means the only disadvantage incurred by the American defense planners. Even more startling was the fact that, after cipher experts had accomplished the almost miraculous feat of breaking the supposedly unbreakable Japanese naval code, some of the decoded intercepts, which pointed plainly to the locus of the attack, were allowed to languish unread in Washington in-baskets. The consequences of this faulty procedure have been set forth in impressive detail by Ladislas Farago, a former naval intelligence officer, in his book *The Broken Seal.* Farago further shows that its primary cause was simply that the intercepts were either considered unworthy of deciphering or, after being deciphered, of being read by responsible officials.

As noted earlier, the striking similarity between Japan's surprise attack on Pearl Harbor and the one launched against Port Arthur in February, 1904, by Admiral Togo has tended to obscure certain other similarities between the two wars which go much deeper. In 1904 the problem had been to gain control of the Sea of Japan, so as to ferry an army to the mainland. The army's function would then be to take Mukden before a new fleet could be sent out from Russia. In 1941 the problem was on a vastly enlarged scale but otherwise much the same. The object now was to knock out the U.S. Pacific Fleet and then, before the U.S. could replace it, distribute army garrisons throughout a vast area in the South Pacific. The supplies of oil and other essentials they acquired would make it possible to stand off the counteroffensive when it finally came. While obviously risky, this plan was by no means a harebrained gamble. If, as then seemed possible, Germany eventually gained a stalemate in Europe, it was entirely conceivable that the Japanese could make their Far East empire virtually invulnerable to a counterattack within a space of two or three years.

Japan's original plan for gaining control of the South Pacific had been to entice the U.S. Fleet to venture forth from Pearl Harbor and then to ambush and annihilate it, as completely as Togo had annihilated the Russians at Tsushima. The idea of copying his opening gambit at Port Arthur rather than his tactics at Tsushima was even more daring but also one that offered even greater rewards if it succeeded. The author of the battle plan was the onetime ensign Isoroku Yamamoto who had lost two fingers of his left hand serving on the battleship *Nisshin* at Tsushima and who was now the commander in chief of Japan's Combined Fleet. However, while prepared to risk all on this opening move he was by no means sure that, even if successful, it would lead to eventual victory. Asked by Prime Minister Konoye what Japan's chances would be in a war with the United States, Yamamoto offered a guarded reply: he foresaw success for a year or two, "but after that I am not at all sure."

Often quoted as having boasted that he "would dictate the peace treaty in the White House," Yamamoto was portrayed by American war propaganda as one of the most bloodthirsty members of Japan's warrior clique. Actually, like most of Japan's top admirals, he was far more dubious about his country's prospects than her generals, of whom many regarded Europe's defenseless Far Eastern colonies as "prizes left lying in the street to be picked up." Yamamoto was a Harvard graduate and had served during the twenties as naval attaché in Washington, where he had learned not only to enjoy bridge and poker but also a good deal about America generally. While many members of the army "Control Group" were inclined to consider the United States to be, like Russia in 1904, a feckless monster rent by internal dissension and incapable of resolute action, Yamamoto held an opposite view. What he had actually said about the White House was that if Japan expected to win, she must be prepared to fight until the United States was obliged to sign the peace treaty there. The success at Pearl Harbor did little to change his mind.

From a Japanese viewpoint, the attack on Pearl Harbor had, in fact, been much less successful than it might have been. While four of the eight U.S. battleships in the harbor had been sunk and the remaining four seriously damaged, all three aircraft carriers attached to the U.S. Pacific Fleet had been elsewhere at the time—one en route to Australia, one carrying planes to Midway, and one in San Francisco— and these had been the major objective. Japanese losses had been trivial—less than 100 dead, five midget submarines, and 29 planes out of 423—but this was in part because the planes had departed without trying to demolish U.S. fuel storage tanks and repair docks, an omission which was later to prove costly. In any event, Yamamoto's initial comment on the action was one that later proved to be an accurate summing up: "I fear," he said on learning that the bombs had started to fall fifty-five minutes before the declaration of war, "that all we have done is to awaken a sleeping giant—and fill him with a terrible resolve."

Japan's scheme for a Greater East Asia Co-Prosperity Sphere called for hegemony over French Indochina (later to become North Vietnam, South Vietnam, Laos, and Cambodia), Thailand, Burma, Malaya, the Philippines, Borneo, the Celebes, and the Indonesian islands of Sumatra, Java, and western New Guinea, along with the adjacent seas and all the island groups and chunks of the mainland already in her possession at the time of Pearl Harbor. This was a gigantic empire covering an area—albeit mostly composed of water—larger than any other previously assembled including that of Genghis Khan. Plans for acquiring it included not only the attack on Pearl Harbor but also coordinated campaigns in the Philippines, Burma, and Malaya.

When Thailand, already outflanked by the previous Japanese move into Indochina, submitted to occupation, Japanese troops promptly began to pour down the west coast of Malaya toward Singapore. Built as a naval base to withstand any conceivable assault from the sea, Singapore was hopelessly vulnerable to land attack. After Japanese planes had sunk the battleships *Prince of Wales* and *Repulse* during their efforts to prevent troopships from landing on the Malayan coast, Japanese ground forces had little difficulty in reaching the narrow strait separating Singapore from the peninsula. The base could put up little resistance and surrendered on February 15.

Burma presented somewhat more of a problem, inasmuch as Ran-
goon had been the Allied port of entry for supplies being sent overland
to Chiang Kai-shek via the so-called Burma Road. Nonetheless, despite
a change of British commanders and a skillfully managed retreat by
Chinese forces under U.S. General Joseph Stilwell, the priorities of the
European theater prevented the Allies from providing the reinforcements needed for successful defense. Japan was in effective occupation
of Burma by the end of April.

In the Philippines, where General Douglas MacArthur was fin-
ishing a five-year tour as field marshal of the Philippine Army, he had
been recalled to command the U.S. Army forces in the Pacific during
the summer of 1941. MacArthur's plan for defending the islands,
pending adequate reinforcement from the United States, called for a
holding action in the Bataan Peninsula followed, if necessary, by a
stand in the offshore fortress of Corregidor. With the U.S. Fleet effectively paralyzed by the defeat at Pearl Harbor, there was no way for
reinforcements to reach him. Ordered to leave for Australia, Mac-
Arthur escaped from Corregidor early in the winter, and the fortress
fell, after a heroic defense, on May 6, 1942.

The Japanese theory that, with Holland occupied by German troops,
its exiled government in London would not be able to do much in the
way of defending Java, Sumatra, or the western half of New Guinea
proved to be eminently sound. After the fall of Singapore, much the
same logic applied to such outlying British possessions as North
Borneo, Sarawak, and Hong Kong, although the garrison at the third
had been reinforced by two brigades of Canadian troops a few days
before hostilities began. The net result was that Japan's acquisition of
the biggest empire ever assembled in world history had been completed—with the loss of only 15,000 men, 380 airplanes, and four
destroyers—in less than five months. By this time, however, the sleeping giant referred to by Yamamoto had started to rub his eyes.

Though Japan had acquired its empire even more readily than expected, there remained the problem of defending the huge area
against the inevitable U.S. counterattack. The first step in so doing was
to destroy what remained of the U.S. Pacific Fleet before it could be
rebuilt into an effective offensive weapon. In order to accomplish this,

Yamamoto planned a grand-scale landing on the small island of Midway, a thousand miles west of Hawaii. If the U.S. Fleet ventured forth to defend Midway, it would become an easy prey to his greatly superior force of battleships and carriers; and if it failed to do so, the island itself could become a base from which to mount another and more conclusive attack on Pearl Harbor. The Japanese Fleet, under direct command of Yamamoto on board his 70,000-ton flagship *Yamato,* set out for Midway in late May.

On the morning after the Battle of Tsushima, when Admiral Togo's ships had rounded up the remnants of the Russian Fleet and forced them to surrender, a Russian officer who was taken on board one of the Japanese ships as a prisoner was astonished when he heard her captain order the gun crews to engage in target practice. Why, he inquired, was target practice called for on the morning after one of the greatest victories in naval history? The Japanese skipper, well versed in Togo's theories about such matters, answered by quoting an ancient samurai proverb: "In victory, tighten the strings of your helmet." This was sound advice to which Admiral Yamamoto, although himself a Tsushima veteran, paid inadequate heed at Midway.

Yamamoto's plan, which involved practically the entire Japanese Navy, called for eight carriers carrying more than 600 planes, 11 battleships, 22 cruisers, 65 destroyers, and 21 submarines, along with an invasion force of 5,000 troops on 12 transports. By contrast, the U.S.

From a recruitment poster, to a parting toast, to the final suicidal attack, the kamikaze *pilots embodied the ancient warrior ethic of a fight to the death.*

had a total of 76 ships of which only three were carriers, and one of these was *Yorktown,* hastily patched up after serious damage in the Battle of the Coral Sea a few days earlier. The Japanese plan was to open the engagement with a smaller diversionary landing in the Aleutian Islands of which the main purpose was to lure the Pacific Fleet northward from its base in Hawaii. If this succeeded, the Americans would be caught between the diversionary force and the Japanese main body under Admiral Nagumo which could then finish off the job started at Pearl Harbor. If the Pacific Fleet did not venture forth to defend the Aleutians, it might still try to come to the defense of Midway, and meet much the same fate.

What Yamamoto did not know was that, with somewhat closer attention now being paid to intercepted Japanese code messages, this entire plan was well known to Admiral Chester Nimitz at Pearl Harbor. Japanese overconfidence during the early phases of the battle—of which Walter Lord's *Incredible Victory* provides a superlative account—was revealed in several instances, but one alone would have been sufficient. When the take-off of a scout plane from the heavy cruiser *Tone* was delayed for half an hour by a faulty catapult, Nagumo decided to gamble on the probability that there was no U.S. striking force in the area thus exempted from surveillance. Despite the consequent risk to his carriers, he ordered torpedo planes on two of them to be rearmed with bombs for an air strike on Midway.

In fact, the segment of ocean omitted from his search was the one in which Admiral Raymond Spruance with his carriers was lying in wait for the Japanese. The delay in launching the *Tone* search plane gave Spruance the jump on his opponent. By the afternoon of June 4, the four best Japanese carriers had been sunk, the landing force had been withdrawn, and the tide of the war in the Pacific had turned forever.

Along with Stalingrad and Alamein, Midway can be counted as one of the three great decisive actions of World War II. Had the Japanese destroyed the last U.S. carriers and effected a successful landing on this minute island, they might well have been able to occupy the Hawaiian Islands before the U.S. could launch a new fleet to defend them. This in turn would have enabled them to cut U.S. communications with Australia and thus conceivably to have held on to their new empire long enough to make it virtually impregnable.

What happened instead is too well known to require more than rapid summary. Restored to control of the mid-Pacific, the U.S. was able to mount a counteroffensive long before Japan was ready to defend the vast perimeter of her recent gains. While MacArthur's ground forces pried their adversaries out of New Guinea and then worked their way northward, Nimitz's carriers pushed westward across the Pacific via Tarawa, Kwajalein, and the Marianas, until the two forces joined in the Philippines. There, at Leyte Gulf, in the greatest combined air and sea battle ever fought, the Japanese Navy—still in forlorn search of a decisive victory like Tsushima—was itself virtually demolished.

By this time, the U.S. had a total of one hundred large and small aircraft carriers while the Japanese were down to four. Eighty per cent, or some three million tons, of the Japanese merchant shipping which was to have been the means for supplying the newly acquired island bases and for bringing their stores of oil to the homeland, had been destroyed by U.S. submarines and air power. U.S. planes had shot down the one in which Isoroku Yamamoto was flying over the Philippines, killing the commander in chief. These developments set the stage for the final U.S. drive toward Iwo Jima, Okinawa, and the Japanese home islands.

Whatever else can be said about Japan's performance in World War II, it served at least to give the rest of the world considerable new data on that perennially fascinating subject, the Japanese character. While the nations of western Europe had been squabbling with each other on a neighborly basis since the dawn of history and had thereby, along with their derivatives in the New World, come to know each other fairly well, no Western nation except tsarist Russia had ever opposed the Japanese on a large scale. Thus everything about the way Japan started, fought, and ended the war was an educational experience for the West and one which wholly failed to coincide with the concept of Japan as some sort of quaint survival from an earlier period in social evolution.

One obvious example was the way in which prisoners and the natives of occupied territory were treated by victorious Japanese forces. Far from showing excess chivalry, the latter seemed inclined to commit an abnormal quota of atrocities. In view of Japan's reputation for exaggerated politeness, this seemed something of a puzzle. Such books as Ruth Benedict's *The Chrysanthemum and the Sword* later helped unravel the mystery with patient explanation of Japanese concepts like *on* (incurred obligations) and *giri* (reciprocal duties). Nonetheless, it took considerable effort for most Westerners to comprehend that, far from excluding ferocity, Japanese politesse was merely its mirror image and that both were necessary and compensatory aspects of the Japanese psyche. What was equally characteristic in such seemingly contradictory traits was their high degree of intensity.

One reason the Japanese were inclined to disregard the amenities customarily accorded to prisoners of war was, it appeared, that they themselves preferred death to capture. The idea of surrender, indeed, was so foreign to Japanese soldiers that over 25 years after the war's end cave-dwelling holdouts are still being discovered. Even more extraordinary than their lack of consideration for prisoners or for the natives of occupied territories—especially the latter, since Japan was counting on them to see the war as a revolt against European colonialism—were the demands the Japanese made upon themselves.

If anything more than the Japanese attitude toward surrender were required to show the all-out character of Japanese belligerence, it was the performance of the kamikaze pilots in the last desperate months of the war. Warriors of many nations have, to be sure, performed acts of heroic self-sacrifice in the heat of battle, but few have matched this

corps of several thousand otherwise normal young men who undertook quite calmly to dive to a hideous death as human projectiles aimed
at the decks of U.S. warships. Since there was no reliable defense
against this form of attack, the kamikaze did in fact inflict serious
damage on the U.S. Fleet and would doubtless have inflicted much
more in the event of an actual invasion of the home islands.

To American war planners, another painful surprise was the quality of Japanese materiel. In the prewar years, while buyers in the
United States and elsewhere were prepared to admit that the Japanese
could turn out fine silk, porcelain, and potted plants, the idea com-
monly held was that most of their other products were either flimsy
imitations of Western models or even shoddier indigenous knickknacks. "Made in Japan" had become in America the familiar slang
phrase for anything that didn't work properly or broke at a touch.
The idea that a nation which produced such trash could also make
guns that would shoot straight, fighter planes that could outmaneuver
American ones, or, most impossible of all, full-size warships—the
manufacture of which was considered the final test of an industrial
society—seemed utterly preposterous.

In actual fact, as early as the 1870s, most Japanese traders had con-
cluded that their opposite numbers from the United States and Europe
were in most cases tasteless bargain hunters interested only in the
cheapest merchandise available. Instead of trying to tempt such visitors with fine wares which they were equipped neither to appreciate
nor to pay for, the Japanese merchants sold them inexpensive trinkets
especially made for the export trade and sometimes referred to in a
slang phrase as "Yokohama *muke*," or Yokohama junk.

The skillful workmanship and brilliant engineering which, in the
postwar years, was to give "Made in Japan" a new and wholly favorable connotation were, during the twenties and thirties, monopolized
by the army and navy. The craft and precision that had made samurai
swords the world's best had comparable results when applied to modern weaponry. At the start of the war, Zero fighter planes were much
more efficient than anything the U.S. put up to oppose them and, even
at the end, almost as good. Where the Japanese went wrong about
armaments was not in producing poor quality but in letting their
enthusiasm for the very best run wild. Thus *Yamato* and *Musashi*,

Wearing masks and holding hands, school children hurry to an air-raid shelter.

each 70,000 tons and carrying nine 18-inch guns, were undoubtedly the biggest and most powerful battleships ever built anywhere. The only trouble was that, by the time they were launched, they were already almost as obsolete as samurai swords; Japan would have been much better advised to maintain her lead in aircraft carriers of which in 1941 she had ten to the three that were all the U.S. could spare for the Pacific.

One other surprising quality, less apparent to the armed forces of her enemies than high quality material or intensity of combative spirit in the field, was the apparently limitless resilience of Japan's home front. When the capture of the Marianas and the complete disintegration of the Japanese Air Force placed the whole country at the mercy of U.S. land-based bombers, the systematic destruction of her cities began in earnest. Two massive air raids on Tokyo in the spring of 1945 caused 100,000 deaths mostly from suffocation in firestorms like those which followed the 1923 earthquake. Still it was not this, nor the atomic bombs that obliterated Hiroshima and Nagasaki with equivalent death tolls, nor the threat of imminent invasion which caused the Japanese people to accept surrender. It was a few words from their emperor, that far from imperial, let alone divine, figure—and even these were enough to cause an armed rebellion in protest.

Shortly after Japan's capitulation and the appointment of Douglas MacArthur as supreme commander of the Allied Occupation, the latter directed that the emperor personally command all his forces everywhere to cease hostilities. In his *Reminiscences,* MacArthur explained his action by referring to an incident when, as aide to his father, the official U.S. observer of the Russo-Japanese conflict, he visited a Japanese infantry unit stationed near Mukden in 1904. "It was here that I first encountered the boldness and courage of the Nipponese soldier. His almost fanatical belief in and reverence for his Emperor impressed me indelibly. The Second Japanese Army, under General Yasukata Oku, was afflicted by the dread disease of beriberi [it is caused by vitamin deficiency—the Japanese polish their rice, thereby losing vitamin B_1 in the husk]. The surgeon prescribed a prophylactic put up in a small tin can with the inscription, 'To prevent beriberi take one pill three times a day.' Soldiers are much the same throughout the world: they took the pill once, spat it out, then dumped the can into the mud. The surgeon was at his wit's end until some bright young officer suggested that the cans be marked, 'To prevent beriberi, *the Emperor desires you* to take one pill three times a day.' The result was instantaneous. Not a pill was wasted. Nothing but death itself could stop the soldiers from taking the medicine."

This passage provides not only an interesting clue to the means by which peace was restored to the Far East in 1945 but also a striking demonstration of the for-the-sake-of-a-horseshoe-nail theory of human events. Had MacArthur failed to accompany his father to Mukden or, while there, neglected to read and remember the inscription on the tin of beriberi pills, history might well have taken a very different turn in the summer of 1945. However, even the most cursory study of happenings during the latter period also brings to notice numerous other instances wherein hundreds of thousands of American and Japanese lives hung on equally fortuitous trifles. In retrospect, what may seem even more amazing is that General MacArthur ever got the chance to apply his knowledge of what the emperor meant to Japan—or even that Japan ever got the chance to capitulate, thereby enabling him to apply it.

First signs that Japan might be ready to make peace became visible in February, 1945, when, at the instigation of the emperor, preliminary moves were made, first through the Russian ambassador in Tokyo and then through the Japanese ambassador in Moscow, to get the U.S.S.R., as a "neutral power," to act as an intermediary with the Western Allies. As might have been predicted, this somewhat naive gambit proved thoroughly ineffective. So far from performing as a peace intermediary—although a splendid opportunity was provided by the Yalta Conference later that same month—Premier Stalin chose the latter meeting as the appropriate place in which to promise that—in exchange for the Kurile Islands, Sakhalin, and a free hand in Manchuria—the U.S.S.R. would declare war on Japan three months after the European war ended. In early April, he honored this bold assertion of willingness to share in the spoils by announcing that the U.S.S.R. intended to terminate the neutrality pact with Japan that had been signed in 1941.

Termination of the neutrality pact coincided with the first U.S.

landings on Okinawa and helped bring about the fall of the Cabinet headed by General Kuniaki Koiso who had replaced General Tojo the year before. Koiso's successor was Admiral Kantaro Suzuki—the former grand chamberlain who had so narrowly escaped assassination in 1936 and who was the first member of Japan's pro-peace faction to head a cabinet since Prince Konoye. However, Suzuki's tentative moves toward peace, which presently included negotiations with America's Allen Dulles through the Japanese Embassy in Switzerland, also came to nothing. Not until the end of May, when F.D.R.'s personal envoy, Harry Hopkins, flew to Moscow to consult with Stalin about future developments, did the latter, at his third meeting with his American visitor, even acknowledge that "peace feelers" were being "put out by certain elements in Japan." Without bothering to explain that the "certain elements" involved were the responsible officials of the Japanese government, he went on to remind Hopkins of what the U.S.S.R. expected to gain from declaring war and to assure him that, by August 8, Russia's armies on the Eastern Front, reinforced by troops he no longer needed in Europe, would be poised to invade Manchuria.

The dilemma that confronted Suzuki in carrying the negotiations further was caused in part by the vagueness of the Allied demand for "unconditional surrender" which in turn involved his own duty toward the emperor. To the armed forces in the field, acceptance of such terms would seem a complete betrayal of this duty and might lead, among other things, to the refusal of commanders and troops in the field to abide by them, with foreseeable consequences for Allied prisoners of war in their charge. This dilemma was partially solved on June 20

Soldiers bowing before the emperor's palace in deference to his authority

when the emperor himself, at a conference with the six members of the Supreme War Direction Council, took matters into his own hands and gave a direct order: "You will consider the question of ending the war as soon as possible."

On hearing this, the prime minister, the foreign minister, and the navy minister expressed readiness to accept unconditional surrender without more ado. The other three—the army minister and both the army and navy chiefs of staff—were still in favor of continuing resistance until they could get some notion of what "unconditional" really meant. If, for example, it meant extermination of the entire population, it would be preferable to die fighting. If it meant the execution or even the summary removal of the emperor, much the same answer would apply.

After further discussions of this point, it was decided to inform Moscow directly and officially that "the Emperor is desirous of peace," and to send Prince Konoye there to negotiate. The message reached Stalin just as he was setting off for the Potsdam Conference with Harry Truman, who had succeeded F.D.R. on the latter's death in April, and Winston Churchill, who was about to be replaced by Clement Attlee through a general election. This time, the Russian dictator went so far as to mention the matter to Churchill, causing the latter to suggest to President Truman that it might be well to clarify the meaning of "unconditional surrender." By now, however, another matter had arisen to take priority in the minds of at least the United States and British parties to the discussions. This was the atomic bomb.

The successful test of the bomb at Alamogordo, New Mexico, had

occurred while the Potsdam meeting was still going on. When word of the explosion reached Truman and Churchill, the latter informed Stalin in somewhat guarded terms that the U.S. had "a new weapon of unusual destructive force," watching with interest to see how the Russian dictator would react to the news. "If Stalin had had any idea what an atom bomb was, or that the U.S. had been trying to make one, my words would have been enough to make his ears prick up like this," Churchill was later to say, accompanying his remark with an appropriate gesture. Instead, the Russian dictator merely replied in perfunctory tones that he was always glad to hear about such developments and hoped that the United States would make "good use of it against the Japanese."

According to Churchill's memoirs, there was never any reservation whatsoever in anyone's mind at Potsdam about dropping the bomb on Japan as soon as possible. In fact, several of President Truman's top advisers, most notably Fleet Admiral William D. Leahy and Secretary of War Henry L. Stimson, had strong misgivings on humanitarian grounds, reinforced by their conviction that a surrender could be extracted without using the new weapon. However, none of the parties to the discussion knew how the emperor of Japan felt on the latter crucial phase of the question. His message to Moscow had by now received a cool reply indicating that it was too vague to require action on Stalin's part let alone elicit his agreement to receive Prince Konoye. Instead, on the afternoon of August 8, Foreign Minister V. M. Molotov received the Japanese ambassador and read him the U.S.S.R.'s declaration of war upon Japan. Meanwhile, on August 6 the B-29 *Enola Gay* had dropped an atomic bomb on Hiroshima, killing some 80,000 of its inhabitants and maiming innumerous others. On August 10, a similar bomb was dropped on Nagasaki, with comparable consequences.

On July 26 the U.S. Office of War Information in Washington had broadcast the Potsdam Declaration stating that, after unconditional surrender, Japan would not be "enslaved as a race or destroyed as a nation" and would be permitted "to maintain such industries as will sustain her economy." However, no mention was made of what remained the essential point so far as the Japanese Cabinet was concerned. This was still the fate of the emperor, about which considerable disagreement existed in the United States. There for many weeks, such knowledgeable dignitaries as Harry Hopkins, Dean Acheson, and Archibald MacLeish—the latter had visited Japan for a few weeks in 1931 to gather material for an article in *Fortune* magazine—had been urging that the "imperial system" be abolished. The main reason that U.S. views on this subject were not made clear in the Potsdam Declaration was simply that President Truman had not made up his mind— and that no one in Washington really knew enough about Japan to realize that this was all that was holding up the arrival of peace.

In Tokyo, the news of the Russian declaration of war—which arrived in the form of a broadcast from Moscow—had even more impact on the deliberations of the Cabinet than the bomb that had fallen on Hiroshima. Convinced now that there was no conceivable hope of final victory, the members nonetheless remained unable to agree upon some way in which to accept the Potsdam Declaration with the reservation that the emperor be allowed to remain. Again, it was left to the emperor himself to end the impasse. At a meeting of the full Cabinet held in the late evening of August 10, the foreign minister moved that Japan "accept the Allied Proclamation" on condition that *kokutai*—an untranslatable idiom meaning something like "national essence"—could be maintained. Prime Minister Suzuki broke all precedent by asking His Majesty to express his own wishes in the matter. The emperor, who had theretofore refrained from interfering in the deliberations of his ministers, rose to his feet and in a shaking voice gave his "sanction to the proposal to accept the Allied Proclamation on the basis outlined by the Foreign Ministers."

In Washington, the first indication of Japan's decision was a message, sent out in English Morse code by the Domei News Agency to avoid the delay of diplomatic channels, in which acceptance was made contingent on the understanding that the declaration did not prejudice "the prerogatives of His Majesty as a sovereign ruler." When this was brought to President Truman, he summoned Admiral Leahy, Secretary Stimson, Secretary of State James F. Byrnes, and Secretary of the Navy James V. Forrestal, and asked them whether they thought he should accept the offer. Three of the four were in favor of doing so. Byrnes was reluctant on the ground that, if any conditions were to be accepted, "I want the United States and not Japan to state the conditions." The

OVERLEAF: *A residential district of Tokyo almost completely leveled by bombs*

president reached no definite conclusion but instructed Byrnes to draft a reply pending receipt of the official version of the offer. When the official version arrived through the Swiss Embassy, Byrnes brought it to the White House along with his draft reply in which the fate of the emperor was at last spelled out. It was that "the authority of the Emperor and the Japanese Government to rule the state shall be subject to the Supreme Commander of the Allied Powers," with "the ultimate form of the Government of Japan" to be "established by the freely expressed will of the Japanese people."

In Tokyo this message was subject to further objections from the army and navy chiefs of staff. It did not provide for the ultimate fate of the emperor, and there were other ambiguities that might be interpreted to his disadvantage. When these were being explained to the emperor by his keeper of the privy seal, the emperor cut him short: "That's all beside the point. It would all be useless if the people didn't want an Emperor. I think it's perfectly all right to leave the matter up to the people."

At the next Cabinet meeting, this decision by the emperor was approved and arrangements were made for a reply to be dispatched to the embassies in Sweden and Switzerland for transmission to the United States. The only question now was how the decision should be made public in Japan. It was agreed that, since news of the capitulation would seem credible only if it came from the emperor himself, he should record an imperial rescript which could then be broadcast to the entire nation.

Even this plan created difficulties. First there was the matter of exactly how the emperor could explain a surrender since, despite Russia's invasion of Manchuria and the hideous suffering caused by the bombings, nothing in the official communiqués even in the last few days had led the nation to suspect that the war was lost. The euphemism chosen to meet this difficulty was possibly the most amazing understatement of all time: "the war situation has developed not necessarily to Japan's advantage." The emperor then went on to the heart of the matter: "We have ordered the acceptance of the Joint Declaration of the Powers. . . . We have resolved to pave the way for a grand peace for all the generations to come by enduring the unendurable and suffering what is insufferable. . . ."

Before the rescript could be broadcast, word of its contents became known to a group of army officers led by the war minister's brother-in-law and a few kindred diehards who felt that the Cabinet was dominated by peacemongers whose influence on the emperor must be broken. In an effort to prevent the broadcast, on the afternoon of August 14 the leaders of this group contrived to kill the commander of the army division guarding the imperial palace and occupy the office building of NHK, the Japanese Broadcasting Company, from which the recorded transcript would be broadcast. The next morning, military police succeeded in overcoming the attempted coup, whose two leaders then committed seppuku in front of the imperial palace. At noon, the NHK announcer introduced the record: "This will be a broadcast of gravest importance. Will all listeners please rise. His Majesty the Emperor will now read his Imperial rescript to the people of Japan. We respectfully transmit his voice."

In the air raid shelter under the imperial palace the emperor listened to his own voice as the record started: "After pondering deeply the general trends of the world and the actual conditions obtaining in our Empire today, we have desired to effect a settlement of the present situation by resorting to an extraordinary measure. . . ."

CHAPTER VIII

SHOGUN
FROM WEST POINT

While attending a New York dinner party in 1946, Winston Churchill was asked what he considered to be the outstanding accomplishment by any commander during World War II, he replied: "MacArthur's landing in Japan, with such a small force of troops, in the face of several million Japanese soldiers who had not yet been disarmed."

MacArthur's landing took place at Atsugi Airport, some fifteen miles west of Yokohama at 2 P.M. on August 30, 1945. He had left his Manila headquarters the night before and then, after an overnight stop at Okinawa, had taken off for the last lap of his three-year journey north. With him in his new C-54 plane, the *Bataan,* were his personal pilot, Lieutenant Colonel Weldon F. ("Dusty") Rhoades, his chief of staff, General Richard Sutherland, and a few other top officers including Major General Courtney Whitney, to whom the commander in chief, while pacing up and down in the cabin, dictated a list of things to do in Japan after arriving:

"We must first destroy the military power. . . . Then we must build the structure of representative government. . . . Enfranchise the women.

American soldiers' appreciation of some of Japan's charms was one of the first visible steps in renewal of friendship between the two nations.

. . . Free the political prisoners. . . . Liberate the farmers. . . . Establish a free labor movement. . . . Encourage a free economy. . . . Develop a free and responsible press. . . . Liberalize education. . . . Decentralize the political power. . . ."

At the moment there were in Japan only a few thousand U.S. soldiers—practically all members of the 11th Airborne Division, who had been landed there that same morning. Facing them were over 2,500,000 fully armed troops of the Japanese home army; and twenty-two divisions of these were within fifty miles of Atsugi Airport, the home base of the kamikaze pilots whose leader had committed seppuku only a few days before. MacArthur was well aware of the emperor's surrender broadcast two weeks earlier and fully confident of the effect it must have had on most of his subjects. However, he also knew that efforts had been made to prevent the broadcast and that kamikaze pilots had subsequently dropped leaflets over Tokyo to say that the broadcast had been ill-advised and that the population should fight on until the bitter end.

MacArthur knew that the *Bataan*'s arrival might well touch off a last-minute uprising on the part of the army die-hards who would consider it their duty to the emperor to assassinate the leader of the first invasion force to set foot on Japan since the thirteenth century. Unescorted by fighter planes of any sort, the *Bataan* reached Atsugi a few minutes ahead of schedule. As it circled above the field so as to touch down at the appointed time, MacArthur, puffing on his corncob pipe, said to his fellow passengers, "We come as conquerors—and we must show no fear."

On hand to greet the commander in chief was General Robert L. Eichelberger, the commander of the Eighth Army of which the 11th Airborne Division was a part, and the division's own commander, Major General Joseph ("Jumping Joe") Swing, both of whom had arrived a few hours earlier. MacArthur's first words on Japanese soil were addressed to the former, his top field commander throughout the campaigns since 1942: "Bob, from Melbourne to Tokyo is a long way, but this seems to be the end of the road."

One of the ablest authorities on the U.S. occupation of Japan, and the author of a volume of memoirs dealing with the subject, is Dennis McEvoy, who arrived in Japan as a correspondent shortly after the

surrender and stayed on to launch a Japanese edition of *Reader's*
Digest, revive the U.S. Chamber of Commerce, and become a confidant to both the supreme commander and the long-time Prime Minister Shigeru Yoshida. According to McEvoy's account of what followed, an advance party arriving the day before had ordered the Japanese to provide transportation from Atsugi to the Grand Hotel in Yokohama where MacArthur planned to stay until the signing of the surrender on board the U.S.S. *Missouri* in Tokyo Bay three days later. As things turned out, the most serious hazard confronting the new arrivals was the unreliability of the vehicles which the local chief of police had assembled in response to this order. These included an ancient Lincoln limousine for the commander in chief, some rickety prewar sedans of assorted makes for his subordinate generals, and, to lead the procession, a battered bright red fire engine equipped with bells and a siren. The fire wagon presently broke down and held up the odd procession for half an hour until it was laboriously pushed off the road.

Along the highway on either side was posted an armed honor guard of two Japanese divisions whose members stood with their backs to the passing entourage, on the alert for snipers or other potential assassins. Interspersed with these were troops of the 11th Airborne, also fully armed, who stood facing the road, with their backs to their recent enemies. After winding through the ruins of burned-out Yokohama, the straggling line of vehicles finally drew up at the door of the Grand Hotel, a solid stone building which, like the U.S. Consulate a few doors away, had survived the fires and still stood almost undamaged, facing Yokohama Bay across a small park. MacArthur was welcomed by the hotel's owner, Yozo Nomura, who then escorted him upstairs to Room 315, where he was to sleep, and 316 and 317, which were to serve as temporary offices. Nomura some years later was to recall of his distinguished visitor that, "although his eyes flashed impressively, he made no comment about his rooms."

The occupation of Japan by the U.S., which began that afternoon and was to last for the next six years, rates as one of the strangest episodes in world history. For reasons previously noted, the two nations principally involved differed from each other perhaps more thoroughly than any two others on the face of the globe. Also, the occupation itself differed completely from innumerable comparable ventures both in its methods and its basic purposes. Other occupations have customarily had as their objectives exacting some form of retribution from the native inhabitants. The objective in Japan, as somewhat vaguely defined in the Potsdam Declaration, was a far more ambitious one: to reform the Japanese nation from top to bottom in such a fashion that it would hereafter be able to live at peace with all of its neighbors but most especially with the one which was to do the occupying.

As indicated by MacArthur's list of things to do, this was a fairly large order to begin with but it was further complicated by circumstances which might well have daunted a less self-confident commander in chief. These included the destruction of all of Japan's major cities except Kyoto; the economic prostration of the entire population whose average annual income, when the Occupation started, had sunk to the unbelievable figure of $27 per year; the obstructive attitude of the U.S.S.R. which, emboldened by its success in taking over most of eastern Europe after the defeat of Germany, had comparable plans for Japan; and finally the apparent eagerness of numerous bureaucrats, in the U.S. State Department and elsewhere, to utilize Japan as the laboratory for some sort of social experiment along lines of their own devising.

MacArthur's difficulties with the Washington bureaucracy began only a year or so later, when civilian administrators began to arrive on the scene in large numbers. His troubles with the Russians came sooner but these were at least substantially diminished when President Truman, profiting from his knowledge of what the U.S.S.R. was by then up to in East Germany, made it clear that Japan was not to be similarly partitioned. Meanwhile, the immediate problem of feeding the Japanese population was solved, at least in part, when MacArthur ordered that, instead of living off the country as is customary in such circumstances, the occupying army would not only subsist on its own rations but feed the starving Japanese as well, starting off with 3,500,-000 tons of reserve supplies built up in the Pacific area for the anticipated invasion.

When requested by the House Appropriations Committee in Washington to explain his use of army supplies to feed the conquered nation, MacArthur explained that the United States was just as responsible for

the population of Japan as the Japanese had been for their 25,000
U.S. prisoners on Bataan. That the Japanese had mistreated the latter
hardly gave the U.S. the right to do likewise to the 75,000,000 Japanese
after the war was over. He added with characteristic emphasis that
"To cut off Japan's relief supplies in this situation would cause starvation to countless Japanese—and starvation breeds mass unrest, dis-
order and violence. Give me bread or give me bullets."

Among many things that helped the Occupation get off to a good
start was perhaps the not altogether superficial similarity between the
MacArthur regime and the system under which Japan had lived for
a thousand years prior to the arrival of Perry. By retaining both the
emperor and the entire Japanese civil establishment, MacArthur had
placed himself in a position analogous to that of the shogun in former
days and this facilitated his acceptance as a *de facto* ruler both by the
Japanese government and the general population. His objective, to
be sure, was to democratize Japan but the style in which he went about
doing so gave the massive Dai Ichi Building, where the U.S. flag flew
less than a mile from the imperial palace, very much the recognizable
character of a contemporary bakufu. However, the MacArthur regime
differed widely from the shogunate in the spirit of understanding and
mutual respect which came to exist between the commander in chief
and the emperor; and this was perhaps also the most important element of all in making the whole enterprise turn out so well.

Insofar as appearance, personal background, and what is currently
called life style were concerned, it would have been difficult to find
two more thoroughly dissimilar specimens of the human race. The
small, dumpy, owl-eyed Hirohito, born in 1901, had been scrupulously
trained for his future responsibilities first by General Nogi and then,
after the latter's suicide to honor the death of his emperor in 1912, by
Admiral Togo. The future ruler's lifelong devotion to marine biology
was not the only consequence of his long and close association with
the old naval hero. Another was devotion to England, where Togo
had put in the last, and by no means least influential, years of preparation for his own future career.

Curiosity implanted by his tutor helped account for Hirohito's visit
to England in 1921, an excursion unprecedented for any heir to the
Japanese throne and one which, as he was to recall when he visited

London again a half century later, provided the happiest experience of his life. While there, the thing that most impressed the solemn and naive little visitor was his almost too dazzling confrontation with his royal contemporary, the lighthearted and unrestrainedly high-spirited Edward Prince of Wales. On his return to Tokyo, Hirohito brought back—along with a fondness for British breakfasts of bacon and eggs, instead of the fish soup and rice customary even for royal Japanese— a forlorn enthusiasm for several of his dashing young host's favorite pastimes, such as playing golf and drinking Scotch whisky.

Neither of these new interests flourished after his return to the austerity of the moated palace in Tokyo. One mildly riotous evening of toping with some Japanese scions, in faint emulation of the night life habitually enjoyed by Prince Edward, led only to a severe and disheartening rebuke from old Prince Saionji. After diligent golf practice on a private course specially installed on the palace grounds, Prince Hirohito felt ready for a round with his idolized opposite number when the latter paid a return visit to Japan in 1922, but this too turned out much less happily than he had hoped. Judging hastily on the basis of his host's proficiency, the Prince of Wales not only failed to suspect that Hirohito had spent months preparing himself for their royal twosome but even that he had ever before tried to play golf at all.

The subsequent sequestered years in Tokyo, through which tiresome ceremonials had alternated with happy hours in his marine laboratory or on the muddy deck of a seagoing harbor dredge, had perhaps done equally little to prepare His Majesty first for the tense months preceding Pearl Harbor and then for the horrors of a disastrous war entered upon against his own intuition by his militaristic advisers. Now, with a sudden peace bought, on his unwonted initiative and at the price of an unheard-of capitulation, His Imperial Majesty, with no precedents of any kind to guide him and no advisers left whom he could really trust, found himself in a hopeless quandary.

Quandaries were something which, so far as anyone can judge, were totally foreign to the character and even the capacities of General Douglas MacArthur. Grandson of a distinguished jurist and son of a renowned general, he had outshone both in an incomparably brilliant military career, starting with his graduation from West Point at the top of his class in 1903. Commander of the Rainbow Division in

From chopsticks to artfully potted cactuses, native Japanese products found ready foreign markets, thus spurring rapid economic recovery after the war.

World War I, superintendent of West Point in the early twenties, and chief of staff under both Herbert Hoover and Franklin D. Roosevelt, who had broken precedent to keep him on for an additional year, MacArthur had capped his cosmopolitan military record with his sojourn in Manila as field marshal of the Philippine Army. These qualifications, combined with earlier service in the Far East and the victorious campaigns of World War II, made him seem almost providentially well-suited for the post of supreme commander for the Allied Powers during the Occupation.

Six feet tall, strikingly handsome, immaculately dressed, and always flamboyantly self-assured, MacArthur was given to expressing himself in a pontifical style of which he provided a succinct example when asked by an aide why he did not immediately summon the emperor to his office. MacArthur replied:

"To do so would be to outrage the feelings of the Japanese people and make a martyr of the emperor in their eyes. No, I shall wait and in time the emperor will voluntarily come to see me. In this case, the patience of the East, rather than the haste of the West will best serve our purpose."

MacArthur's move from the Grand Hotel in Yokohama to the U.S. Embassy in Tokyo took place on September 8. Along the twenty miles of roadway, bordered by burned-out shacks and workshops, the populace stood cheering as though to greet the return of a victorious Japanese conqueror, in a way that amply verified MacArthur's original thesis deduced from the tin of beriberi pills. Soon after moving in, MacArthur's prognosis was confirmed by polite enquiries from officials of the court as to when the supreme commander could conveniently receive His Majesty. The date and place set for the call were September 26 and the embassy residence, rather than MacArthur's official headquarters at the Dai Ichi Building.

Wearing a cutaway coat, striped trousers, a top hat, and old-fashioned high-button boots, the emperor stepped out of his ancient limousine to be greeted by MacArthur's military secretary, Brigadier General Bonner Fellers, who shook his hand and escorted him to the elevator. Of the conversation between the emperor and General MacArthur which followed—Mrs. MacArthur and their son Arthur peeked through the curtains at the end of the room but they were out of earshot—no official record exists. MacArthur's memoirs, however, contain an enlightening account of the interview which proved to be the first of many.

"He was nervous and the stress of the past months showed plainly. I dismissed everyone but his own interpreter, and we sat down before an open fire. . . . I offered him an American cigarette, which he took with thanks. I noticed how his hands shook as I lighted it for him. I tried to make it as easy for him as I could, but I knew how deep and dreadful must be his agony of humiliation. I had an uneasy feeling he might plead his own cause against indictment as a war criminal. There had been considerable outcry from some of the Allies, notably the Russians and the British, to include him in this category. . . .

"My fears were groundless. What he said was this: 'I come to you, General MacArthur, to offer myself to the judgment of the powers you represent as the one to bear sole responsibility for every political and military decision made and action taken by my people in the conduct of the war.'

"A tremendous impression swept me. This courageous assumption of a responsibility implicit with death, a responsibility clearly belied by facts of which I was fully aware, moved me to the very marrow of my bones. He was an Emperor by inherent birth, but in that instant I knew I faced the First Gentleman of Japan in his own right."

One of the few Japanese myths more astonishing than the one about the Sun Goddess Amaterasu is the one, so firmly adhered to by many Westerners, that contemporary Japanese themselves believe in it. In fact, even the least knowledgeable Japanese have long since looked askance at this colorful fable while their more sophisticated compatriots have proposed a likely explanation of it. This is that the tale was concocted by the early rulers of Yamato soon after the art of writing became popular, in order to substantiate their own primacy, and was later perpetuated by Shinto priests for similar reasons. That Japanese reverence for the emperor as a ruler goes back only to the Meiji restoration is suggested by the fact that, during the late Tokugawa period, Townsend Harris had lived near Edo for some years before he even learned that there was such a thing as an emperor.

Theretofore, Harris had heard of him only as "some sort of pope" who lived in Kyoto.

Since, of all Japanese, the one who believed least in the divinity of the emperor was naturally Hirohito himself, he was the first to welcome the chance to dispel any lingering doubts upon the subject, albeit more for the benefit of credulous foreigners than for his own subjects. When he gathered from his advisers that a few words to this effect would be very much in order, he lost no time in providing them by way of a New Year's Proclamation on January 1, 1946.

"We stand by the people and we wish always to share with them in their moments of joys and sorrows. The ties between us and our people have always stood upon mutual trust and affection. They do not depend upon mere legends and myths. They are not predicated on the false conception that the Emperor is divine and that the Japanese people are superior to other races and fated to rule the world."

The emperor's New Year's broadcast made headlines all over the world and was widely hailed, in the United States especially, as marking the dawn of a new era in Japanese culture. However, if any Japanese were much surprised by the sentiments expressed, history has failed to record it.

With relations between himself and the emperor amicably adjusted and the food problem well in hand, MacArthur wasted no time in getting down to the main business of the Occupation. As a specialist in doing first things first, he gave a high priority to the question of who was going to run Japan and soon settled this in characteristic style. According to an agreement reached by Secretary of State James Byrnes in Moscow in December of 1946, final authority for the Occupation was to be something called the Far Eastern Commission, composed of representatives of all eleven nations that had engaged in the war, which would meet in Washington. Its recommendations would then be transmitted to the four-power Allied Council for Japan in Tokyo, comprising representatives of the U.S., Britain, China, and the U.S.S.R., which would transmit them to MacArthur.

In practice, since MacArthur was on the spot and since each of the four major powers on the Far Eastern Commission in Washington could veto all the others, nothing was ever decided either there or by the Allied Council. If only by default, sole power resided in the supreme commander for the Allied Powers, or SCAP, as his headquarters came to be called. How MacArthur used this power was clearly shown by a passage in his *Reminiscences* describing one of his early meetings with the Soviet delegate to the Allied Council, a burly and loquacious general named Kusma Derevyanko:

"The Russians commenced to make trouble from the very beginning. They demanded that their troops should occupy Hokkaido, the Northern Island of Japan, and thus divide the country in two. Their forces were not to be under the control of the Supreme Commander, but entirely independent of his authority. I refused point blank. General Derevyanko became almost abusive and threatened that the Soviet Union would see to it that I would be dismissed as Supreme Commander. He went so far as to say that Russian forces would move in whether I approved or not. I told him that if a single Soviet soldier entered Japan without my authority, I would at once throw the entire Russian Mission, including himself, into jail. He listened and stared as though he could hardly believe his own ears, and then said politely enough, 'By God, I believe you would.' He turned and left, and I heard nothing more of it. But the Soviet had other ways of carrying out his threat against me. It took several years but their day finally came."

With the Russian problem at least temporarily disposed of, the next item on the list was completing the demobilization of the 6,983,-000 Japanese soldiers on the home island and elsewhere who still remained under arms. A million and a half of these, comprising the so-called Kwantung Army which had opposed the U.S.S.R. on the borders of Manchuria, disappeared into Soviet or Chinese Communist captivity and were not heard of again for several years. Thereafter, a few thousand survivors, having first been subjected to thoroughgoing Marxist indoctrination, were allowed to trickle back in small groups, apparently in the hope, which proved unjustified, that they would then stir up insurgency among their compatriots. Meanwhile, the dismantling of the remainder of the vast Japanese war machine, including military installations and storage facilities, was entrusted to the Japanese Army and Navy ministers, working under the supervision of SCAP officials and with the help of the Eighth Army and the U.S. Navy. The job was to all intents finished by the end of October.

Speedy demobilization of Japan's armed forces through the agency of Japanese officials was to set the keynote for the subsequent operations of SCAP in other directions as well. Retaining the emperor and the entire apparatus of government made Japan's administrative bureaucracy in effect an arm of the Occupation. This arrangement enabled SCAP to accomplish, rapidly and with an amazing economy of means, a vast catalog of reforms which, if the Occupation had set up an alien administration of its own, would have been wholly unthinkable. Under MacArthur's system, the total number of occupation-duty troops in Japan never much exceeded some 40,000 prior to the outbreak of the Korean War.

Before the Occupation was two months old, MacArthur himself issued a "Civil Liberties Directive" whereby all restrictions on political, civil, and religious rights then in force were removed, all press censorship cancelled, all political prisoners released, and the thought control police summarily abolished. This proclamation in itself knocked down with one blow the elaborate artifice which it had taken the militarists half a century to construct and which had kept the entire country almost as ignorant about what was really going on in the world—including major developments in World War II—as it had been under the Tokugawa. However, this was only the beginning; even more alarming charges were to follow.

In MacArthur's dual role as commander in chief of the U.S. Armed Forces in the Pacific as well as supreme commander for the Allied Powers, most of his functions in the former capacity were delegated to General Eichelberger as commander of the Eighth Army. Meanwhile, his obligations under SCAP were entrusted to three main sections, each of which was headed by an old MacArthur associate and staffed by civilian specialists. The latter were supplied, mostly through the State Department, from the ample manpower bank in Washington.

Of these three sections, the most controversial was that responsible for the economic and scientific area of Japanese affairs, headed by General William Marquat who had served under MacArthur since the days of Bataan. According to the terms of the Potsdam Declaration, one of its two main functions was "breaking up" the zaibatsu which had previously controlled some 80 per cent of the whole Japanese economy. The other was to "purge" from high posts in Japanese

Signs in both English and Japanese flash in Tokyo's bustling Ginza district.

finance, industry, and commerce all executives who had cooperated with the military in planning and running the war. Both these objectives were based on the dubious premise that Japan's business community had eagerly aided and abetted the militarists from the outset, whereas in fact most of them had been, at the worst, reluctant accomplices. An additional disadvantage was that in her grim economic straits after the war, Japan needed all the managerial expertise that could be rounded up. Nonetheless, Marquat's section forged boldly ahead on both fronts, purging thousands of Japan's ablest executives and removing from control of the pulverized zaibatsu the managers and directors who, with their forebears, had built these organizations over the course of decades or even centuries.

Never much in favor of this basically unfair and vindictive operation, MacArthur nonetheless felt obliged to let it proceed under the supervision of his trusted subordinate "with as little harshness as possible." Under these circumstances, dispossessed zaibatsu shareholders were bought out at reasonable figures and the various divisions of the great combines allowed to carry on as best they could. As things turned out, they did far better than might have been expected and even the purging process may have served a useful purpose in helping develop new young executive talent. MacArthur's later comment in his memoirs reveals his attitude toward the whole procedure:

"The punitive feature of such a policy always outweighs all other attributes and invariably breeds resentments which carry the germs of future discord. Many of those involved are patriots who serve their country in the light of existing conditions, and their punishment makes personal expiation for the mistakes of the nation. As soon as the peace treaty restored Japan's full sovereignty, all prohibitions against the purgees were promptly, and properly, removed."

Top priority for the Government Section under Brigadier General Courtney Whitney, a onetime Manila lawyer and MacArthur's closest confidant, was provision of a new constitution in time for a national plebiscite scheduled for April of 1946. When the first draft prepared by Japanese Cabinet members proved to be a mere rewrite of the 1889 one, save for minor variations such as the substitution of "supreme" for "sacred" in describing the position of the emperor, a team of government section rewrite men under General Whitney was assigned the task of providing a totally new one. The result, after a week of furious creative activity, was that a more up-to-date document, based partly on U.S. and partly on British models, was completed in time to meet the deadline for the national plebiscite, which heartily endorsed it. After a year of study and debate, the Diet gave its approval; and the new constitution took effect in May of 1947.

Unlike the procedures of the Economic and Scientific (E & S) Section, those of the Government Section in most cases stood the endurance test provided by the subsequent peace treaty and remain in effect today. Contrary to common supposition, the constitutional provision renouncing war as an instrument of Japan's national policy was not part of the version prepared by U.S. specialists. It was proposed earlier by the then prime minister, Baron Kijuro Shidehara, and endorsed by MacArthur as a means of preventing the military from ever trying to resume power, of assuring the rest of the world that Japan sincerely intended never to wage war again, and of relieving the nation of the burden of maintaining expensive armaments which it was in no position to afford. The no-war clause has thus far proved acceptable on all three counts but especially on the third, since the absence of military expenditures has been an important factor in Japan's postwar economic recovery.

In pre-World War II Japan, one sign of the influence of the military upon primary-school thought patterns was that when six-year-old girls jumped about on hopscotch squares, they customarily did so in time to rhymes extolling the 1905 exploits of General Nogi and Admiral Togo. Textbook arithmetic problems dealt not with apples and acres but with troop movements and supplies of munitions. Under Brigadier General Kenneth R. Dyke, a former New York advertising executive, and his successor, Lieutenant Colonel Donald Nugent, a teacher in prewar days, the Civil Information and Education (C I & E) Section set about rectifying such martial overemphasis by a stupendous rewrite program. In this, the members of Japan's teaching profession and publishing industry cooperated so eagerly that within a year 250 million new textbooks had been printed and distributed. Meanwhile, responsibility for the control of Japanese educational policy was removed from central bureaucratic control in Tokyo and assigned to prefectural governments and local school boards.

Educational reform, the new constitution, and the dissolution of the zaibatsu were only a few of the earliest and most spectacular accomplishments of the Occupation. Others included extensive legislation designed to encourage the growth of labor unions and limit the power of employers; far-reaching land reform, intended to release farmers from the onerous rents imposed by absentee landlords; and voting privileges, presently accompanied by new job opportunities for women which equaled, if they did not exceed, those available in the United States or Europe. Along with all this, despite the emperor's plea that he be held solely accountable for the actions of all his subordinates, went the trials of war criminals which, while they attracted little attention from the Japanese public, were conducted with as much equity as could reasonably have been expected from such legally questionable tribunals.

To imply that such innovations which, over a period of five years, were to change Japanese life to a degree comparable with that effected by the Meiji restoration or the civil wars of the twelfth century were accomplished without vast turmoil, conflict, and confusion would be wholly misleading. The reverse was the case, within both the Occupation government and the resident community. Fairly typical of confusion in the latter category was an incident resulting from the election of April, 1946, when a legislative leader called on General MacArthur to report an alarming crisis in the Diet. As reported by the supreme commander himself, the caller, when asked to provide details of the crisis, replied with some embarrassment:

" 'A prostitute, Your Excellency, has been elected to the House of Representatives.'

"I asked him: 'How many votes did she receive?'

"The Japanese legislator sighed, and said: 'Two hundred and fifty-six thousand.'

"I said, as solemnly as I could: 'Then I should say there must have been more than her dubious occupation involved.'

"He burst into a gale of laughter. 'You soldiers!' he exclaimed, and dropped the subject. . . ."

The troubles among the Americans began with a large infusion of bureaucrats in the spring of 1946. Many of these held vaguely Marxist theories about human nature in general and government administration in particular which, as intermittently implemented mainly by the C I & E and E & S sections, sometimes produced incongruous results. One of these was a series of strikes encouraged by E & S although they impeded Japanese economic recovery at a time when millions of people were homeless or starving. Another was the development, with C I & E's apparent approval, of strong Communist influence in both the Japanese Teachers' Union and the student organization called *Zengakuren,* whose frenetic riots antedated the world-wide student revolts of the sixties by a full decade.

Despite such unhappy exceptions, it can be said that on balance the U.S. Occupation of Japan was a huge and astonishing success. The sheer novelty of the whole proceeding helped divert the minds of the population from the incredible hardships they were obliged to undergo in the first years after hostilities ended. Far from resenting the presence of the conquerors who had invaded their whole heretofore sacrosanct country, the Japanese behaved as though getting the U.S. Army to come there had been their primary war aim all along. Venerable zaibatsu chiefs listened attentively to juvenile SCAP bureaucrats who lectured them on the sins erroneously supposed to have been committed by their vast combines; diligent workmen, happy in their chores, flung down their tools and tried valiantly to quarrel with their bosses under urgings from the Labor Division of the E & S Section; small children lined the smoky streets of ruined suburbs cheering the GIs who roared past in their jeeps and screeching, "Hello, hello!" aptly mispronounced as "Hero, hero!"; and a famous geisha named Momoya-san, or Honorable Peach Blossom, reputed to be the most beautiful and talented in Tokyo's Shimbashi District of the Flower and Willow World, became so popular with Occupation hosts after *Life* magazine ran her picture that she learned English, took up golf, and eventually came to New York to run a thriving tempura and sukiyaki restaurant.

To serious students of the Occupation, the risk inherent in the whole operation seemed to be that the Japanese might wind up with the notion that democracy itself, if that was what it was all about, was a kind of crazy charade, only practicable under the aegis of some indulgent alien shogun. Since they apparently wanted nothing so much as to learn all they could from their conquerors, their intense cordiality

toward the latter might well be understandable, but what was going to happen when MacArthur went home, taking all the friendly American mentors with him? That question was, in due course, to receive an unexpected answer.

Theories on how long the Occupation should continue naturally differed widely. A consensus of U.S. authorities at the outset might have guessed at ten years, but others—including many underlings of SCAP itself, who perhaps felt reluctant about abandoning the fine houses and numerous servants made available to them—thought that true repentance might require several decades or maybe even a round century. MacArthur, whose military style was marked by a strict economy of means, had much less grandiose ideas. At a luncheon at the Tokyo Foreign Correspondents' Club in March, 1949, he dropped a minor bombshell by suggesting that to all intents and purposes the main part of the Occupation's job had already been completed and that the time was now at hand to draft a peace treaty and get out.

Right: Emperor Hirohito pays a formal call on General MacArthur. Above: a much lighter side of the American Occupation is documented.

The Foreign Correspondents' Club in Tokyo was a somewhat raffish establishment on the corner of Shimbun, or Newspaper, Place, often referred to as Shinbone Alley by club members who spent much of their time tossing dice for drinks in the bar, like their colleagues at the National Press Club in Washington. The latter was a far more dignified institution whose membership included most of the major journalistic pundits in the capital. Many of these were on hand at noon on January 12, 1950, when Secretary of State Dean Acheson gave a luncheon address which naturally got considerably wider coverage than MacArthur's earlier off-the-cuff remarks in Tokyo.

In the course of his address to the Press Club in Washington, the secretary spelled out the Far East situation in considerable detail. The U.S., he explained, had a strategic line of defense in the Pacific. This line did not include Korea or Taiwan. To make his point completely clear, the secretary, as later recorded in his autobiography, went a little further by saying:

"So far as the military security of other areas in the Pacific is concerned, it must be clear that no person can guarantee these areas against military attack. . . . Should such an attack occur . . . the initial reliance must be on the people attacked to resist it and then upon the commitments of the entire civilized world under the Charter of the United Nations. . . ."

In order to get the full impact of this statement by the U.S. secretary of state, it is useful to have in mind the background of events prior to and between the two lunch-time Press Club addresses. During the early years of World War II, when it might have been easy for Generalissimo Chiang Kai-shek to have made peace with Japan on favorable terms, he had continued to fight on virtually alone, thus pinning down some 1,200,000 Japanese troops that would otherwise have been available for use against the U.S. At the November, 1943, meeting between Roosevelt, Churchill, and Chiang Kai-shek in Cairo, it was agreed that after the war "all the territories Japan has stolen from the Chinese, such as Manchuria, Formosa (Taiwan) and the Pescadores, shall be restored to the Republic of China. . . ." What happened after World War II instead was well summed up by a young veteran of the fighting in the Pacific named John F. Kennedy in January, 1949, just after his election to Congress:

"During the post war period began the great split in the minds of our diplomats over whether to support the Government of Chiang Kai-shek or force Chiang Kai-shek as the price of our assistance to bring Chinese Communists into his government to form a coalition. . . . The continued insistence that aid would not be forthcoming unless a coalition government was formed was a crippling blow to the National Government. So concerned were our diplomats and their advisers . . . with the tales of corruption in higher places, that they lost sight of our tremendous stake in a non-Communist China."

In February, 1949, a month or so later, fifty-one congressmen asked President Truman to explain U.S. policy in China. Truman, whose famous definition of the presidency was "where the buck stops," on this occasion passed it to Secretary Acheson, whose answer to the question was to become almost equally celebrated. U.S. policy in the Far East, he said, was "to wait until the dust settles." By February a year later, when the secretary made his address to the National Press Club, enough dust had settled on, among other things, the graves of several million Chinese "bourgeois reactionaries" to give his more specific appraisal of geographic priorities considerable significance.

Shortly after the secretary of state's speech to the Press Club, General MacArthur invited him "to be my guest in Tokyo. I had never met Dean Acheson, but felt certain that his survey of the Asiatic situation would materially alter his expressed views. He declined the invitation, saying that the pressure of his duties prevented him from leaving Washington. He did, however, visit Europe eleven times during his stay in office."

While Russia had failed to get possession of Hokkaido as a zone of occupation analogous to East Germany, agreement had been reached at Yalta—the previous agreement with Chiang Kai-shek to the contrary notwithstanding—to hand over the northern half of Korea. The line blithely chosen as the boundary between the United States and Soviet zones for no good reason that anyone ever took pains to elucidate was the 38th parallel, which crosses the waist of the peninsula just north of the ancient capital at Seoul. In South Korea, the aging patriot Syngman Rhee, who had been exiled from his homeland by the Japanese takeover of 1910, became prime minister after the election of 1946. In North Korea, where no election was held, the Soviet authorities set about turning the territory into an armed camp. There, by the spring of 1950, 200,000 well-drilled indigenous troops were ready for action.

To say that Secretary Acheson's Press Club speech in February of that year provided these troops with a green light for aggression, as many of his critics have subsequently suggested, may well do its author an injustice. Nonetheless, if its intention was to provide anything in the nature of a deterrent, his rhetoric proved woefully ineffective. On June 25, as soon as the spring rains were over and the season appropriate for a rapid advance toward the south, North Korean armies smashed across the lightly defended border.

For military historians the Korean War, which ended in a stalemate, provides several points of special interest, as do the differences in policy between MacArthur, as commander in chief of the United Nations forces which opposed the Communist invasion, and the State Department in Washington, which issued directives on the subject. However, the pros and cons of such matters can best be examined in the memoirs of the personages involved and other relevant material. For the purposes at hand, the main point is that argument between Washington and MacArthur wound up in the latter's finding out, from a news broadcast on the Tokyo radio, that he had been summarily relieved of all duties in the Far East and that his military career had come to an abrupt conclusion.

For the past five and a half years, MacArthur had been ruling Japan with an authority unparalleled by any shogun or emperor. Thus, while he had been preaching democracy, what he had been practicing was, in the very nature of his job, precisely the opposite. The sudden discovery that this dread personage, whose slightest whim had had the effect of absolute law, was himself subject to the whim of a remote and relatively unknown dignitary elected by American voters was almost as much of a shock to the Japanese public as its earlier discovery that Japan had lost the war. All the more because of the rudeness with which it was accomplished, MacArthur's dismissal showed, as nothing else could possibly have done, what democracy was really all about. Winston Churchill's apt comment upon MacArthur's unceremonious arrival in Japan—as quoted in the general's memoirs—would perhaps have applied even more aptly to his even less ceremonious departure.

In a broadcast to the nation, Premier Shigeru Yoshida paid a tribute which, coming from the head of state to the departing commander in chief of an occupying army, may well be unique in history:

"The accomplishments of General MacArthur in the interest of our country are one of the marvels of history. It is he who has salvaged our nation from post-surrender confusion and prostration, and steered the country on the road of recovery and reconstruction. . . . It is he who has paved the way for a peace settlement. No wonder he is looked upon by all our people with the profoundest veneration and affection. I have no words to convey the regret of our nation to see him leave."

Similar messages of sympathy came from the Diet, from heads of neighboring states, and from the Japanese press. To a nation whose militarists had only a few years before been used to telling the population what thoughts to have, however, the amazing thing was to learn how a U.S. soldier behaved in a moment of unimaginable personal defeat. Along streets and roads lined by some two million Japanese, some of them in tears, others cheering and waving, MacArthur and his family drove from the embassy to Atsugi Airport, where he had landed in August, 1945. There government dignitaries were on hand to say good-by and the general calmly took the salute of the Tokyo garrison.

After MacArthur's departure, his titles and duties as supreme commander passed to General Matthew B. Ridgway, who carried the Korean War through to its conclusion in 1953. A peace treaty between the United Nations and Japan was signed in San Francisco in September, 1951, with the U.S.S.R. abstaining. However, to all intents and purposes, the Occupation era had ended five months earlier when, as the sun was rising, MacArthur's plane took off, flew south to circle snow-covered Mount Fuji, and then headed east over the Pacific.

CHAPTER IX

SEIKO TIME
TO SUPER-STATE

P ossibly because in the United States internal competition in various forms is already sufficiently intense to satisfy the normal human urge toward aggression, external warfare has usually been found superfluous. By corollary, when the U.S. does engage in extraterritorial hostilities, its armed forces maintain, insofar as possible, the amenities of peaceful life at home. One means to this end is the Post Exchange, or PX, whose function is to provide troops on alien fronts with tobacco, chewing gum, soda pop, candy bars, shaving soap, and toothpaste. In Japan, where the warriors of the Occupation force had no fighting to do and were in many cases accompanied by their dependents, the typical PX soon evolved into a luxury department store. In order to satisfy the civilian needs of the occupying forces and to help revive the Japanese economy, Occupation authorities first allowed and then encouraged PX managers to stock their shelves with a wide variety of indigenous products. Starting out with silks, folding screens, and tableware, these presently came to include more complicated merchandise, like watches, cameras, and radios.

It was in the PX stores serving the Occupation forces that "Made in

Children in their festival costumes preserve the ancient tradition of Emperor Shomusai's Death Day which includes a parade through the streets of Nara.

Japan" first ceased to be a contemptuous cliché applied to any gadget that failed to work and began to acquire the opposite significance. However, to Japanese manufacturers, the PX trade had advantages far exceeding immediate profits. It gave them both an invaluable cross section of the U.S. market on which to pretest wares for subsequent export and a group of paradoxically "captive" customers—who, on their return to the United States, could be counted on to boost Japanese products.

One good case in point was the Japanese camera, perhaps the first Japanese product to make substantial postwar gains on the worldwide export market. During the Russo-Japanese War of 1904–05, there had been only three pairs of high-grade binoculars in all of Japan. All three came from Germany's Zeiss factory and were brought back to Japan by a titled traveler who gave one pair to the emperor, sent another to Admiral Togo, and kept the third for himself, presumably for purposes of research. By the time of World War II, Japanese lenses were equal to the world's best, but their use was confined to bombsights and range finders for the army and navy. Only after the war, when the Occupation authorized optical manufacturers to retool their factories and rehire their workmen for peacetime production, were such lenses available commercially in field glasses and cameras.

A special factor involved in the success of the cameras was the presence in Japan of numerous professional photographers attached to the international press corps. Not long after the Occupation started, a *Fortune* magazine photographer named Horace Bristol shared darkroom facilities with a Japanese colleague who convinced him and *Life*'s David Douglas Duncan, by optical-bench tests, that Japanese Nikon lenses were equal to those of the visitors' Leicas. Use of Japanese cameras by other top-notch professionals like Alfred Eisenstadt and Carl Mydans in covering the Korean War for mass magazines quickly spread the fame of these instruments around the world and helped accelerate their subsequent popularity.

The saga of Japanese chronometry goes back further than lenses, to the early days of the Meiji period, when a schoolboy named Kintaro Hattori got a job as messenger for a Tokyo shopkeeper whose main item was imported watches. When Hattori later opened a similar shop of his own, one of his customers brought back a broken watch with the request that he repair it. In the effort to comply, the shopkeeper perforce found out what made it tick. By the turn of the century, Kintaro Hattori had become Japan's watch king, and his splendid shop on the Ginza was Tokyo's Tiffany.

During World War II the Hattori Company, like Nikon, was engaged mainly in turning out armament accessories like timing devices for bombs and torpedoes. With their factories bombed out and their work force scattered, Hattori's grandsons made a fresh start during the Occupation. Completely new machine-tool equipment and assembly-line methods, patterned on those of Detroit, enabled them to mass produce the fine jewel-lever watches that had previously been made only by highly paid artisans in Switzerland. Twenty years later, Hattori was producing 15 million Seiko watches a year compared to 55 million watches for all the watch companies in Switzerland, and its complex electric timers had been used with record-breaking success for all events in the 1964 Olympic Games in Tokyo.

Success stories like those of Seiko watches and Nikon cameras were typical of numerous other Japanese companies in the years during and after the Occupation. However, while the marketing and manufacturing methods used by such companies helped explain the flowering of Japan's economic recovery, an even more basic factor in this was the soil in which the flowers grew. This was the Japanese culture in general and the Japanese economy in particular.

Where the Japanese economy differs chiefly from that of other free-world nations is in the relations between its three main components—government, management, and labor. In most developed nations, labor and management are in permanent contention with each other for the profits of production, while government acts as an uneasy and frequently suspect umpire. In Japan, government, management, and labor are, in effect, all players on the same team. Instead of competing against each other, they see their role as helping each other compete against the outside world. This is a totally different viewpoint and one that raises complex questions such as: How did the Japanese acquire it, and how do they actually make use of it?

A good statement about how capital teams up with labor in Japan was provided not long ago by Soichiro Honda, whose company, started on a shoestring after World War II, is now the biggest motorcycle producer in the world. Asked by a U.S. reporter how he avoided laying off workers during a lull in consumer demand, Honda, who spends most of his time in a worker's uniform at a bench in the company laboratory, had a samurai answer: "An employer like me has a job just like everyone else in the plant. It is my job to foresee business trends, make plans to meet them, and thus keep all my men on the job. If I fail to do it, then it is I who should be fired, and not they."

To workers in the United States or Europe, such a response might well sound insincere if not wholly implausible. When told that most workers in Japan expect the kind of job tenure that in the U.S. goes only to vice presidents, full professors, and a few other privileged characters, they suspect a trap of some sort. Fringe benefits customary in Japanese industry such as paid vacations, New Year's bonuses, free medical care, low-rent housing, wage allowances for increase in familial responsibilities, and even in some cases free plots in the company graveyard, sound like evil "paternalism" carried to an unimaginable and horrifying extreme. Japanese workers, however, far from mistrusting paternalism, base their careers on it. What they expect from their bosses is the kind of loyalty that a father gives to his children; they consider it fair to give back filial loyalty in return.

A good illustration of how filial loyalty operates in Japanese companies may be their answer as to how best to assure the quality of goods produced by assembly-line methods, a key question for all industry in the free world. (Since the only effective final check on quality is a competitive market wherein customers can reward high quality by buying it and penalize poor quality by rejecting it, this question hardly arises in Communist economies, which goes far to explain their inability to compete in international commerce.) Like factories elsewhere, Japanese ones use various forms of inspection to detect flaws in their output, but, in addition to these, they have also developed other devices for the same purpose, of which one is known as the Quality Control Circle. A Quality Control, or QC, Circle is a group made up of a dozen or so workers and one or two foremen who meet voluntarily first to discuss and diagnose weaknesses in production and then to find ways of correcting them. The unique characteristic of these circles, of which some 20,000 have sprung up in different industries during the past decade, is that the employees who compose them meet, as a rule, not during work hours but after work, sometimes for half pay but more often for no pay at all.

How effectively such QC circles work was indicated not long ago by a report made to a Quality Control Conference in Tokyo by a circle representing the Matsushita Electric Company, Japan's biggest single manufacturer, concerning a flaw in its car radios. When consumer records showed that some radios were being returned because of loose control knobs, a QC Circle set out to determine whether this was attributable to parts, operators, tools, or work techniques. Its members traced the trouble down to a minute variation in part sizes that was often aggravated by hasty or careless workers; and a fault in the design of the specially shaped screw drivers used in adjusting the knobs. What made the report amazing to U.S. observers was that it was submitted not by highly paid management-oriented efficiency experts, but by three girls off the assembly line, aged 23, 21, and 18.

Said a top U.S. management consultant on quality control named J. M. Juran not long ago in an article for the *Journal of the American Society for Quality Control*: "The Japanese manager has . . . retained his leadership of the work force and not lost it to the union, the politician or the intellectual. . . . In the noncommunist West, the leadership passed to someone else and still rests there. . . . To regain this leadership is a long journey and the present generation of managers will not make it (in my opinion). . . . The Japanese are headed for world quality control leadership, and will attain it in the next two decades, because no one else is moving there at the same pace. . . ."

The QC Circle is by no means Japan's only innovation along these lines. Others are indicative of the way in which government in Japan cooperates with labor and management to further the interests of both. One takes the form of a productivity center in Tokyo, whose purpose is to act as a clearinghouse for information on how to step up production, not in one industry but in all. Another is an export control law, initiated by management and passed in 1956 with the wholehearted backing of labor, whereby all goods for export must pass rigid tests in order to carry the proud label "Made in Japan."

Three-way cooperation in such matters as quality control is merely one small and relatively superficial example of the way in which Japanese government, labor, and management work together like the fingers of a hand instead of fighting each other in a perpetual free-for-all as they do in the United States and Europe. To most Japanese, the Marxist theory that the workers of the world should unite against their employers seems totally absurd. They feel instead that Japanese workers, bosses, and government not only should unite to outproduce the rest of the world but that, with military conquest now effectively ruled out, they *must* do so—and that their individual fate as well as that of the nation depends on how well they do it.

At once the most satisfactory and the most thoroughly Japanese example of how government, labor, and management cooperate to mutual advantage is no doubt that unique institution, the zaibatsu. Often described as "family companies," the zaibatsu have usually been portrayed in the West as gigantic and vaguely sinister cartels, each run by a single despotic clan. Nothing could be further from the truth, as can be readily discerned from a glance at their origins. What happened in Japan was that, instead of nationalizing private enterprise in a mature economy as the government of England has lately done, the Meiji regime got industrialization started by doing exactly the opposite. Since private capital within Japan was practically nonexistent and since it was felt, with ample justification, that importing capital from abroad might lead to foreign domination, the government simply used its tax receipts to start basic industries. Later, when these industries became capable of making profits, they were sold off to private investors at more or less nominal prices.

Prior to World War I, the chief bidders for such government properties were, to be sure, the family proprietors—originally displaced samurai or affluent artisans, who had become financial advisers or bankers to major daimyo. During the eighteenth and nineteenth centuries they built up Mitsui, Mitsubishi, Sumitomo, and Yasuda, the original zaibatsu Big Four. It was these old-line zaibatsu that helped check militaristic adventurism during the twenties although, as the army Control Group acquired power thereafter, a second crop of smaller zaibatsu grew up that thrived mainly on government contracts in armaments and related fields. By the time SCAP instituted its policy of breaking up the zaibatsu, all four of the oldest and biggest had ceased to be actively run by the founding families. Through the well-recognized process of managerial revolution, personal administration

The Japanese have become enthusiastic baseball fans since its introduction in 1873. Here a spectator cheers her team during a hotly contested game.

if not financial control had to a considerable extent passed into the hands of alert young outsiders, leaving the descendants of the founders free to cultivate the arts and dabble in philanthropy, sometimes of a socialist nature, financed by their free-enterprise profits.

By the time the Occupation ended, the zaibatsu had indeed been thoroughly broken up but this was proving to be more of a help than a hindrance in their further evolution. Since the complexities of Japan's vastly expanded post-World War II commerce put a premium on increased flexibility and scope, the net effect was that the splintered segments became in effect incipient zaibatsu on their own, related to each other in a looser and more horizontal organization than the more rigidly structured originals. In consequence of such proliferation, the zaibatsu as regrouped at present are bigger, more versatile, and more effective than ever. The way in which the zaibatsu—whose major field is international trade—work together with Japan's biggest banks, domestic manufacturers, and each other was recently set forth in *Time*:

". . . Presidents of the 27 Mitsubishi companies meet one Friday every month; . . . and the 17 Sumitomo presidents one Monday a month. The big borrowers from the Fuji Bank have a council known as Fuyo Kai, which includes the heads of Hitachi (electrical machinery), Nissan Motors (autos), and Nippon Kokan (steel). The clubs divide up markets like so much sukiyaki. When Communist China recently decreed that it would not trade with Japanese firms that do business with South Korea or Taiwan, the clubs quickly reached an understanding: Mitsui and Mitsubishi decided to concentrate on South Korea and Taiwan, while Sumitomo took China."

To suggest that the cooperation between government, labor, and management is the salient difference between the Japanese economy and all others in the free world is not to imply that this is the sole explanation for the Japanese "economic miracle." Obviously there are innumerable contributing factors, large and small, overlapping and independent, on high level and on low. These include the willingness of Japanese capitalists to take greater risks than most others; of Japanese workers to work harder; and of the Japanese government to comprehend and satisfy the interests of both. However, for the purposes at hand, the important point is not so much to enumerate, let alone to analyze, such individual factors as it is to identify the basic

cause that underlies all of them. What this involves, fortunately or
otherwise, is a further look at that notoriously elusive subject, the Japanese character.

During the nineteen-forties, many U.S. Far Eastern experts felt that Communism would never make much headway in China because of certain ineradicable Chinese characteristics expressed in age-old Confucian doctrine, such as reverence for authority in general and for parents in particular. Events of the next few years were to show that, on the contrary, what twenty centuries of respect for authority had actually accomplished in China was to generate such a profound impatience with parents and all their psychological equivalents that the number of "bourgeois reactionaries" summarily dispatched in the first two years of the Communist revolution is currently put at somewhere between two and ten million. Miscalculations of this kind serve to underline the dubious value of generalizations about all ineradicable national characteristics. Some such traits, like the Chinese respect for parents, prove readily susceptible to abrupt change by political means. Others turn out to depend on mere geographical location, as proved by millions of European immigrants to the United States who have made a point of discarding their national characteristics and acquiring American ones in their place as rapidly as possible.

In the case of the Japanese, such generalizations are, if possible, even less reliable than usual. For one thing, as clearly shown by the behavior of second- or third-generation Japanese in California and elsewhere, few supposedly innate Japanese traits survive transportation to a new locale. For another, as suggested by many incidents in their history, Japanese often fail to behave like Japanese even at home. The best way of explaining Japanese motivations may therefore be to consider some environmental factors involved, starting with education.

Possibly the most striking accomplishment of Japan during the past decade has been her emergence as the world's leading shipbuilder, specializing in wholesale production of 300,000-ton oil tankers, while her previous mentor in such matters, Great Britain, was struggling, with dubious success, to launch a single diminished replica of an old-fashioned ocean liner. One way to account for this accomplishment has been to cite the fact that Japan had already given some indication of her shipbuilding proclivities by constructing such comparatively diminutive vessels as the *Yamato* and the *Musashi*. Another was to point out that, by using high-grade Australian ores that only became available after World War II, Japanese steelmakers have been able to fabricate an alloy more resistant to metal fatigue than any other in the world. A third and perhaps even more fundamental cause, however, was mentioned not long ago by an executive of the Mitsui Shipbuilding Company, one of the nation's largest:

"Courses in naval architecture are provided in most other great ship building nations like England, Sweden and the U.S. at only one university in each. In Japan, four universities—Tokyo, Osaka, Kyushu and Yokohama—each has its own faculty in this discipline. Each awards more degrees in it than each of the single universities in the other nations. The result is that while each of the other countries turns out ten or twenty qualified naval architects a year, Japan turns out over three hundred. This means that a shipbuilding company like ours can employ naval architects three or four deep at levels where other countries are lucky to have one. We have enough naval architects—some 7,500 graduates since World War II—to use the younger ones as plant foremen—nor are they wasted in such posts. Most of the workmen under them are themselves high school, and some of them college, graduates as well."

Japan's output of naval architects is by no means an isolated phenomenon. It is equaled or exceeded by the proportionate output of qualified specialists in every other walk of commercial, industrial, and professional life, nor is this a recent development. For many decades, Japan has claimed a literacy rate of 99 per cent, or the world's highest. Even allowing for some modification of this, to accommodate competing claims from other nations, the Japanese level remains remarkable in view of the fact that Japanese is perhaps the world's hardest language to be literate in. Japan's book publishers produce more new titles a year than those of the United States with more than twice Japan's population. As of May 1, 1969, Japan had a total of 379 universities—more than in all Europe—not to mention another 500 or so college-level institutions of a more specialized type.

Japan's appetite for learning is doubtless one of the main factors in

her present prosperity—just as it was in her great leap forward under
Meiji, whose charter oath included the assurance that "knowledge shall
be sought from all over the world and thus shall be strengthened the
foundation of Imperial polity." However, to cite this appetite as the
basic motivation underlying Japanese behavior patterns would be—
since the appetite is itself such an important element in the patterns—
to beg the essential question. The important thing to find out about
the Japanese is why they are now, and have been heretofore, so peculiarly responsive to, and enthusiastic about, learning things. If we
could discover the reason for this, we might be able to account not
merely for the emergence of a Japanese superstate but also for many
of the previous bewildering oscillations in Japan's astonishing history.
To identify the ingredient that makes the Japanese differ from the rest
of mankind would moreover improve not merely our knowledge of
Japan but also our understanding of mankind in general, including
ourselves.

Unfortunately for patient readers of this book, the sad fact is that,
despite all the brave advances in human knowledge made in the last
two thousand years or so, including the forays by Freud, Pavlov, and
their even more recent confreres, the answers that can so far be provided to such questions are by no means altogether satisfactory. While
the proper study of mankind is no doubt man, the results of research
along this line are still lamentably meager. The best that can be done
in the case of the Japanese may therefore be to offer a few hints for
the benefit of future psychologists and psychiatrists, and even these
hints may not be altogether dependable.

In one of Conan Doyle's most celebrated stories, the discovery that
enabled Sherlock Holmes to solve a peculiarly tantalizing mystery was
that a dog which should have barked failed to do so. A handy point at
which to start unraveling the oddity of Japanese behavior may by
analogy be the familiar truism that Japanese babies do not cry. While
there may be many exceptions to this rule, it is at least undeniable that
most Japanese babies cry much less than most babies elsewhere. If, as
Freud and the Jesuits seem to agree, the first years of a human life are
the ones that do most to form character, this omission on the part of
Japanese infants may perhaps offer a fairly important clue to their
subsequent behavior as adults.

The reason that Japanese babies do not cry is by no means an occult one. It is merely that, whenever they show signs of doing so, their mothers give them whatever it is they want, usually something to eat. The result of this—and of comparable indulgences, such as day-long piggyback rides and sleeping in the same room as their parents—is that infancy for the Japanese is likely to be an intensely satisfactory time of life. Enjoyment of this period, during which the Japanese infants get more lenient treatment than infants anywhere else, may be retrospectively enhanced by the fact that it ends in an exceptionally abrupt transition to the next period, wherein serious, not to say grown-up, duties and responsibilities are suddenly encountered at the age of four or five.

The earliest years of life are those in which any individual, if he is to survive, must acquire certain fundamentals such as the knowledge of how to drink, eat, walk, think, and talk. These are formidable accomplishments and—although most humans are later on understandably inclined to take them for granted—ones that surely involve efforts comparable to any that may later be called forth in acquiring more recondite forms of learning. Where Japanese children differ most notably from other children may be that for them these first efforts in the field of learning are accompanied by unique fringe benefits in the form of infantile pleasure. Pleasure thus becomes indelibly associated with learning as what behaviorists call a "reinforcer"; and learning itself becomes something in the nature of what Pavlovians describe as a "conditioned reflex."

One bit of evidence in support of this theory may be the eager diligence with which Japanese children go about the next major step in their education, which is that of learning to write their own language. According to former U.S. Ambassador to Japan Edwin O. Reischauer—who, having grown up in Japan and learned to write Japanese during his own childhood, can speak with special authority—Japanese small fry are "sentenced to generation after generation of numbing memory work simply in order to learn the rudiments of writing." Actually, the effort that Professor Reischauer, reared in the household of a distinguished Presbyterian missionary, recalls as being painful may possibly have seemed much less so to his small Japanese contemporaries. In any case, the effect of learning to write Japanese upon young Japanese

—and even its effect upon the erudite and versatile professor himself—
would certainly appear to have been anything but numbing.

Taking a view divergent from that of Professor Reischauer, some
other educators have argued that, just as learning Latin and Greek used
to be accepted as the best way for juvenile Europeans to develop intellectual muscle, so learning some two thousand ideographs may provide an even more effective type of mental gymnastics for toddlers in
Japan. According to this theory, the main reason that adult Japanese go
on learning things so eagerly is that, once having learned how to write
Japanese, any other accomplishment along educational lines becomes
effortless by comparison. This line of thought, however, seems pertinent only until one recalls that it was the characteristic Japanese appetite for knowledge that caused the nation to take up Chinese calligraphy to begin with.

Adopting, then, the hypothesis that the Japanese eagerness to learn
stems from a process of identifying enjoyment itself with anything that
serves to re-create in the subconscious the delicious luxuries of the
prerecollective period of infancy, there is considerable supporting evidence to be found in fields outside that of education. Among the

The bunraku, *or puppet, theater, which predates the kabuki, has remained popular with the Japanese. Here a cast of characters awaits its next performance.*

"innate" character traits that Westerners are likely to notice first about the Japanese are, for example, their enthusiasm for, and expertise concerning, not only giant oil tankers but also all sorts of certifiably minute things, such as bonsai, haiku, netsuke, not to mention transistors, tiny watches, and, most recently, cassette tape recorders; their propensity for forming groups and the wholehearted acceptance by such groups of parental substitutes on almost any level, such as the factory foreman, the company president, or the "divine" emperor; their tendency to worry more than most people do about what "other people" will think of them; and, finally and above all, their capacity for sudden and unpredictable changes in all behavior patterns, including those just mentioned.

However, even if these patterns are assumed to be, in one way or another, continuations of or reversions to the characteristics of earliest childhood, nothing could be more erroneous than to infer that Japanese adults are handicapped by some sort of infantile approach to life. What the assumption might suggest is rather that, on the contrary, Westerners may be handicapped by having lost—perhaps by too much discipline at the outset of their careers or too little later on—most of the curiosity, responsiveness, fury, and glee that small children everywhere in the world seem to share but that only Japanese children appear able to carry on into adult life. Putting it another way, Japanese adults seem to have retained, perhaps because of certain parental contributions to their upbringing overlooked by such diverse Western authorities as the revered Benjamin Spock and B. F. Skinner, most of the temperamental virtues of childhood, along with a minority of its temperamental defects.

The hypothesis that Japan's metamorphosis from a nation in abject and unimaginable defeat into the world's third superpower may have taken place—along with many other startling switches in Japanese history—merely because Japanese babies don't cry is, of course, unlikely to endear itself to most Occidental deep thinkers on such subjects. Preferring to ignore the fact that, like most of the other major discoveries in man's study of mankind to date, those of Pavlov, Freud, and others are nothing if not obvious once elucidated, they will prefer to deride such explications for being not merely simple but "simplistic." However, there is no way to prove the point short of mass psychoanalysis, which would be an experiment in education so far never attempted even in Japan; and in any case this book is not a detective story which requires a neat solution in the last chapter. Since most Western academicians will presumably wish to continue thinking of the Japanese as the most mysterious creatures in the whole Mysterious Orient, it may be as well to drop the entire subject at this point and conclude on a more congenial note—that of Japan's immediate future.

According to Herman Kahn, the learned director of the Hudson Institute, in *The Emerging Japanese Superstate,* Japan's Gross National Product by 1980 will be somewhere between 450 and 750 billion dollars a year and by the year 2000 somewhere between 1.5 and 4.5 trillion. Meanwhile per capita income will jump from $2,000 to $10,000 a year. Taking the mean between extremes, the Japanese curve would pass the U.S. curve in per capita income around 1990 and in Gross National Product around the year 2000. However, since all these projections assume that the growth rate of the Japanese economy would have dwindled from its present 10.6 per cent to something between 10.5 and 5.5 per cent per annum, they may fall far short of reality.

Much if not most of this prosperity will have come from increased trade with the non-Communist nations of the Pacific area—Burma, Cambodia, Taiwan, South Vietnam, Hong Kong, Indonesia, South Korea, Malaysia, the Philippines, Singapore, and Thailand. Except for mainland China, these are roughly the same components as those of Japan's proposed pre-World War II Greater East Asia Co-Prosperity Sphere, with which Japan even now does a trade amounting to over 10 billion dollars a year. In short, Japan has already accomplished in less than two decades, by entirely peaceful means and with the full cooperation of all concerned including the United States, precisely what the Pacific war was fought to prevent.

In fact the chief distinction between the Greater East Asia Co-Prosperity Sphere as originally proposed and Japan's present trading area, aside from the means of their attainment, is that the original sphere did not contain either Australia or New Zealand, while the present one includes both. Far from being in any way unwelcome to

OVERLEAF: *Karatsu Castle, Kyushu, situated above a harbor now crowded with a fleet of fishing boats.*

the other nations involved, this new Co-Prosperity Sphere is precisely what its name suggests. The eleven relatively undeveloped nations in the first group now have a rapidly increasing GNP of 62 billion dollars a year and a per capita income of $200. By the year 2000, with the help of Japan as a trading partner, these figures should have increased to roughly one trillion and $1,600 respectively. Meanwhile Australia's and New Zealand's combined GNP should rise from 45 billion to 250 billion and its per capita income from $3,000 to $10,000.

All these estimates are based on dollars at their present purchasing power so that, if present inflationary trends continue, they should be revised even further upward. Where they may perhaps most gravely err on the optimistic side is that they are also based on the supposition, perhaps unjustifiable, that there will be no major nuclear war between now and the end of the century. Since Japan's ability to survive at all, let alone to prosper as at present, depends mainly on foreign trade, such a war would, of course, be for her a total disaster. In any event, a more profitable subject for speculation may be the extent to which Japan's economic role in world affairs can continue to increase without some sort of roughly commensurate increase in her military capabilities as well.

Dismayed by the speed of Japan's economic conquests, American commentators frequently cite as reasons Japan's supposedly low wage rates, and still more frequently the budgetary advantage that Japan receives as a result of the U.S. obligation to maintain Japan's defenses at negligible cost to Japan. While more factually sound than the argument about low wages, which no longer applies, the second argument cuts little ice in Japan. The constitutional provision outlawing war—which, if not actually inspired, was strongly endorsed by the U.S. Occupation—has long since also acquired the full support of most Japanese voters. Appalled at the mess their militarists made of things in the thirties and forties, the Japanese are nowadays equally delighted by the progress made without benefit of armaments in the decades since the war. Left to their own devices, there is little chance that they would wish to get involved in nuclear competition with the world's two military superpowers—with whom anything short of complete parity would be much more of a liability than an asset.

Rather than alter its present "low posture" in respect to defense,

Japan may presently come to terms with the United States on this potentially vexing problem from another direction entirely. One objection to Japan's methods of doing international business frequently voiced by American businessmen is that, while Japan reaps huge profits from its trade with the United States, it bars any meaningful U.S. participation in its own economy through rigid government regulations. Japanese restrictions on foreign capital participation has been based on the understandable fear that this might corrode the tight links of nationalist motivation that now bind Japan's labor, management, and government together. However, a new theory has lately been voiced by some forward-looking Japanese business leaders. According to its foremost proponent, President Akio Morita of Sony, who is also perhaps the most prosperous of all Japan's new generation of major exporters, entrance of U.S. capital into the Japanese economy should be welcomed as a means of insuring the continuation of U.S. willingness to shoulder the burden of Japan's defense. "If we allow more U.S. investment, we will not need a security treaty," says Morita. "Of course the Americans will protect us then. Everybody protects his own property."

In the current state of geopolitical affairs, some compromise along these lines seems a practicable objective for the United States and Japan to work toward through the coming decades. Given the geographical plan of the globe and applying the isothermal theory of population—whereby peoples living close to the equator lack the drive and initiative of those in the temperate zones—current apportionment of power shapes up in a fairly obvious pattern. Discounting Australia, New Zealand, and the relatively small nations occupying the temperate tips of Africa and South America along with the equatorial countries to their north, the power nuclei of the globe consist essentially of the two major blocks, centered in the north temperate zone. One of these, comprising the major Eurasian land mass, includes the U.S.S.R., China, and perhaps eventually India, along with adjacent satellites in Europe and elsewhere. The other is North America with what amount to protecting beachheads on the peninsula of Europe and the fringes of Southeast Asia. The island clusters off the east and west coasts of the world's biggest land mass are thus indispensable parts of the U.S. defensive apparatus. Interior frictions within each of the two major blocks and temporary detentes or accommodations between them may from time to time modify or blur the pattern of relationship. Nonetheless, so long as the world retains anything like its present political alignment, Japan and England will represent in effect the free world's two defensive fists, and the U.S. obligation to insure Japan's security can be more or less taken for granted.

Outside of Japan's defense problems and the continued growth of its economy, the urgent questions that remain are not so much those concerning Japan's own future as those involving its future impact on the rest of the world. To expect the world to trade with Japan on the scale which it seems likely to do without being deeply influenced outside the field of economics would seem highly unrealistic. Nonetheless, before assuming that Japan's current momentum will continue indefinitely and that in the twenty-first century the whole world will be eating with chopsticks, sleeping on *tatami* mats, and dancing to the strains of the *samisen,* it may be permissible to recall that no tree grows as high as the sky and that there still seem to be comparable limitations on the extent of human enterprise.

If, for example, nationalistic unanimity accounts in large part for the cohesive thrust of the Japanese economy, an influx of foreign capital, even allowing for the compensatory advantages cited by Akio Morita, might still have a disrupting effect on this essential motivation. Similarly, if the whole inverted pyramid of Japan's prosperity is really based upon Japanese customs in child rearing, some apparently trifling alteration in these, perhaps to be brought about by the nation's new cosmopolitanism or by other unpredictable changes in social circumstances, might well have a correspondingly adverse effect upon such vital factors as the Japanese worker's attitude toward authority and the closely related one of his willingness to work much harder than workmen elsewhere.

What makes such fundamental alterations all the more conceivable is that what Japan's current economic boom clearly represents is not a mere shift in cultural emphasis but a major structural change, the closest precedent for which may be that of the wars between the Taira and the Minamoto almost a millennium ago. What was at stake then was the question of whether the country was to be run by the intellectuals and aesthetes of the imperial court at Kyoto or by the war lords in the provinces. When the latter won, the result was that militarism

in one form or another remained the keynote of Japan's history until
August 15, 1945.

The stupefying discovery on that day that this time-honored tradition had brought the nation to total disaster went much further than merely disillusioning the Japanese public about the army clique of the twenties or even about the Meiji period before that. It had the ultimate positive effect of elevating to the top of the social order precisely that element in the population that had traditionally been at the very bottom—the despised merchants.

That these merchants have so far done very well is amply proved by the history of the past few years. However, what will determine Japan's future for the long range will be their ability to discharge the responsibilities that were formerly borne by predecessors cast in a totally different mold. Any contemporary effort to predict the results of this abrupt switch would be rash indeed. About all that can be safely said is that such a complete and sudden metamorphosis is entirely consistent with Japanese character—and that like everything else about Japan, its results are quite sure to be well worth watching.

CHRONOLOGY

1688–1704	Genroku period; era of urban culture; flourishing of the romantic novel, *haiku* poetry, and *kabuki* drama
1791–1792	Americans and Russians try to establish trade with Japan
1846	Commodore James Biddle attempts to open Japan to trade
1853	Commodore Matthew C. Perry arrives at Uraga and demands that Japan open her ports to trade
1854	Perry negotiates the trade treaty of Kanagawa
1856	Arrival of Townsend Harris, first American envoy to Japan
1858–1868	Warring factions compete for power
1860	Japan sends its first embassy to the United States
1867–1868	Fall of shogunate; accession of Emperor Mutsuhito Meiji
1868–1912	The Meiji period; the royal capital is moved to Tokyo; Japan rapidly Westernizes; acceptance of foreigners
1871	Postal service founded
1873	Meiji abolishes feudal fiefdoms
1877	The Saigo rebellion; the samurai's last stand
1889	The Meiji Constitution is promulgated
1894–1895	The Sino-Japanese War
1902	Anglo-Japanese Alliance
1904–1905	Russo-Japanese War; the Russian fleet is destroyed at the Battle of Tsushima Strait
1910	Japan annexes Korea
1912–1926	Reign of Emperor Yoshihito
1914–1918	Japan fights in World War I on the side of the Allies
1923	The Great Kanto Earthquake Disaster
1925	Universal manhood suffrage is granted
1926	Accession of Emperor Hirohito
1931–1932	The Manchurian Incident; Japan forms state of Manchukuo
1937	Hostilities with China begin
1940	Formation of the Rome-Berlin-Tokyo Axis
1941	Japan occupies Indochina; signs neutrality pact with Russia; tries to reach a diplomatic compromise with the U.S.; attacks Pearl Harbor; declares war on the U.S.
1941–1945	Pacific War
1945	The U.S. conducts air raids on Tokyo; atomic bombs are dropped on Hiroshima and Nagasaki; Japan surrenders
1945–1951	Allied occupation of Japan under General MacArthur
1950	Outbreak of the Korean War
1951	A peace treaty is signed with forty-eight nations; U.S.-Japan security pact
1952	End of military occupation of Japan by Allied forces
1956	Japan is admitted to the United Nations
1964	The Olympic Games are held in Tokyo
1970	Expo '70 is held in Osaka
1971	U.S. agrees to return Okinawa to Japanese rule

CREDITS AND INDEX

Page numbers in **boldface type** refer to illustrations.
Page references to map entries are in *italic type.*